MW01532403

ALSO BY KEVIN ELLMAN CFP

7 Biggest Money Mistakes and How to Avoid Them

"Kevin Ellman keeps his '7 Biggest Money Mistakes' simple, but not simplistic. From investing to insurance to estate planning, it's all here in an easy-to-read, unintimidating style. Spend an hour – I promise, a single hour, and you'll be smarter and richer for it."

-Tyler Mathisen, CNBC

"Wow! If you only read the first chapter, you are way ahead of the game; but read it all. It's a book for all age groups. This book will prepare you to have intelligent conversations with your financial advisers."

- Phil Fine, Vistage International
Best Practice Chair/Master Chair/Group Chair

"Kevin Ellman has created a great resource for anyone looking to avoid making financial mistakes. Easy to read and follow, this book is a must read for everyone."

-Kathleen Burns Kingsbury,
Wealth Psychology Expert and Author, Breaking Money Silence

"7 Biggest Money Mistakes… is a well written, thoughtful and invaluable tool for people at all stages of their life. He has taken a complicated subject and broken it down into easy to understand strategies. I strongly recommend this book. It is easy to read and a powerhouse of extremely useful information."

-Deacon Bob Duncan, Vistage International
Best Practice Chair/Master Chair

Copyright © Wealth Preservation Solutions, LLC., 2021. All Rights Reserved.
No part of this work may be reproduced in any form without written permission.

Authors: **Kevin Ellman CFP, CEO** and **Paul D. Miller, President**

Wealth Preservation Solutions, LLC.

NEW JERSEY - CORPORATE HEADQUARTERS
45 Eisenhower Drive, Suite 550
Paramus, NJ 07652
T 201.632.2020
F 201.445.6720
Email Kevin Ellman: kellman@wpsllc.net

wealthpreservationsolutions.com

FLORIDA*
725 Hideaway Bay Drive
Longboat Key, FL 34228
T 941.383.4396
F 201.445.6720
Email Paul D. Miller: pmiller@wpsllc.net

DEDICATIONS AND ACKNOWLEDGEMENTS

Sue Forman, of our office, and **Anthony Vitiello**, Chair of Taxation and Estate Planning at Connell Foley, lent their invaluable expertise to the technical aspects of tax management and estate planning.

Belinda Traverso, of our office, shepherded the manuscript through the compliance process.

Ruth Ellman provided professional editorial services, reading, editing and coordinating all aspects of preparing the manuscript for publication.

Book Design and Illustrations: **Janet Atkinson** — janetatkinson.com

DISCLOSURES

The opinions expressed herein are those of the authors and do not necessarily reflect those held by Kestra Investment Services, LLC or Kestra Advisory Services, LLC. This is for general information only and is not intended to provide specific investment advice or recommendations for any individual. It is suggested that you consult your financial professional, attorney, or tax advisor with regard to your individual situation. Comments concerning past performance are not intended to be forward looking and should not be viewed as an indication of future results.

Securities offered through Kestra Investment Services, LLC (Kestra IS), member FINRA/SIPC. Investment Advisory Services offered through Kestra Advisory Services, LLC (Kestra AS), an affiliate of Kestra IS. Wealth Preservation Solutions, LLC is not affiliated with Kestra IS or Kestra AS. Neither Kestra IS nor Kestra AS provide legal or tax advice and are not Certified Public Accounting firms.

[1] As of Dec. 31, 2019, assets include Kestra Investment Services, LLC, Kestra Advisory Services, LLC, Kestra Private Wealth Services, LLC, and Kestra Institutional Services
[2] As of 10/31/2020.
*Paul D. Miller

Fidelity Investments and Fidelity InstitutionalSM (together "Fidelity") is an independent company, unaffiliated with Wealth Preservation Solutions, LLC (WPS). Fidelity is a service provider to WPS. There is no form of legal partnership, agency affiliation, or similar relationship between your financial advisor and Fidelity, nor is such a relationship created or implied by the information herein. Fidelity has not been involved with the preparation of the content supplied by WPS and does not guarantee, or assume any responsibility for, its content. Fidelity is a registered service mark of FMR LLC. Fidelity InstitutionalSM provides clearing, custody, or other brokerage services through National Financial Services LLC or Fidelity Brokerage Services LLC, Members NYSE, SIPC. 887667.2.0

Investor Disclosures

Back in the day, I made a living as a Rock and Roll drummer who played with such music greats as Bette Midler, Manhattan Transfer, Todd Rundgren, Barry Manilow, Chuck Berry and Richie Havens.

This was great training for becoming a 360° Family Wealth Manager.

Why?

In the same way that a professional musician must listen, be sensitive to the other musicians in the band, and allow the conductor to unify the performers, a 360° Family Wealth Manager must listen to a family's vision, be sensitive to their various needs, and coordinate the family's team of advisors to help them achieve their goals.

~ Kevin Ellman CFP, CEO
Wealth Preservation Solutions, LLC

Contents

Introduction 6

What is 360° Family Wealth Management? 7

360° Family Wealth Management 10

The 360° Six-Step Family Wealth Management Process 11

Wealth Preservation 20

The Fate Of The Family Business 21

Wealth Preservation Mistakes Of The Rich and Famous The Miami Dolphins 23

Where Do You Want Your Assets To Go? 25

Federal & State Estate Taxes 29

Why An 'I Love You Will' Is Not Enough 31

The Tax Sensitive Will — Protect Your Assets 33

Estate Equalization 39

Wealth Transfer Planning Tools — Benefits of Hopping the Tax Fence 43

Levels of Wealth Transfer Planning 49

Investment Management 52

Strategies To Help Maximize Your Money 53

Risk Management 64

Life Insurance — The 'Unloved' But Effective
Wealth Preservation and Wealth Transfer Tool 65

Family Business Strategies — Exit and Succession Planning 70

Family Business Strategies 71

The Heir Not So Apparent — Giving Up Shares Without Giving Up Control 73

An Incomplete Plan Does Not Work 75

I Didn't Quit, You Fired Me! 77

Dad, You Are Fired! 79

Make Sure Your Key Executives Don't Leave When You Need Them Most 81

The Golden Handcuffs Program 83

Improperly Designed or No Buy-Sell Agreement 85

Buy-Sell Agreements — What Should They Cover? 87

Types Of Buy-Sell Agreements 93

Buy-Sell Agreements Certificate Of Value — What Is The Buyout Price? 97

Buy-Sell Agreements — Failure To Coordinate 99

Philanthropy 102

360° Family Foundation Management 103

Advisor Coordination 106

The Importance of Overseeing and Coordinating
Wealth Transfer Planning Components and Advisors 107

The Passing Of Assets 109

Pulling It All Together 112

Hypothetical 360° Family Wealth Management Case Study 113

Conclusion 120

360° Family Wealth Management 121

Take The 360° Stress Test 122

About the Authors 124

What is 360° Family Wealth Management?

360°

WEALTH

A Personal Family Office

PRESERVATION SOLUTIONS

360°

What is 360° Family Wealth Management?

Almost every family office we encounter has done some level of Wealth Preservation and Wealth Transfer Planning, using a diverse cast of excellent professionals. They have Attorneys, Accountants, Bankers, Insurance Agents, and Stockbrokers. Typically, they work with each professional at different times over the years as legal and financial issues arise. They do their taxes with their CPA, write a will with their Lawyer, borrow money from their Bank, buy life insurance from their Insurance Agent, and make investments via their Stockbroker.

We call this *piecemeal and incomplete planning.* In a vacuum, each separate, financial or legal element of the plan may be well-crafted. However, there is a risk that this fragmentary approach will create additional problems and costs as a result of poor coordination. More often than not, piecemeal planning creates a new problem for every problem that it solves.

Imagine you want to build your dream home from the ground up. You feel you have a pretty good vision of your ideal house, so you go out and hire a landscaper, carpenter, electrician, plumber, mason, roofer, and pool installer. You tell them what you want and ask them to go to work. How likely is it that you will end up with your ideal house? Not likely at all! An all too common consequence of failure to coordinate is not only ending up with a less than ideal plan but creating costly potential pitfalls.

A better idea, as we all know, is to hire an architect to develop a detailed plan and then supervise its implementation via the general contractor and various subcontractors. This arrangement is much more likely to succeed in achieving the desired result.

In this same way, someone on a Family Wealth Management Team must serve as the architect. For our purposes, we will refer to this role throughout the book as your **360° Wealth Manager**. The role of the 360° Wealth Manager can be fulfilled by different types of professionals, such as Wealth Managers, Financial Planners or Accountants.

360° Family Wealth Management begins by our guiding and helping you bring into focus a vision for your business, your family, and your future legacy.

Once we have developed an agreed upon plan, we oversee its implementation in six distinct but interrelated areas:

- ✓ *Wealth Preservation*
- ✓ *Investment Management*
- ✓ *Risk Management*
- ✓ *Family Business Strategies*
- ✓ *Philanthropy*
- ✓ *Advisor Coordination*

We work closely with your team of advisors to design and implement the plan, and just as important, we help keep the plan on track over time, as your business and family grow, and needs or circumstances change.

All six planning areas must come under the purview of a team of professionals supervised and coordinated by a 360° Wealth Manager, to be maximally effective, and reflect a Family's vision through a well-crafted and executed Wealth Preservation and Transfer Plan.

Occasionally, a family may decide to keep one or two aspects of the plan separate, in effect, saying that they prefer 270-degree or 180-degree planning only. Partial adoption is never as effective as embracing the full 360° program. Inevitably, there will be a failure on some level due to imperfect coordination, and the family may not experience the desired results. In our view, the 360° planning approach provides the best opportunity for implementing and maintaining a successful Family Wealth Management Plan.

Lack of coordination is just one example of the kinds of issues that confront families of wealth. Throughout this book, we will use a combination of case studies, and in-depth examination of the various planning tools, strategies and techniques that can be employed to help reduce or even eliminate the potential damaging effects of poor Wealth Preservation and Wealth Transfer Planning. Let's begin by examining our *360° Six-Step Family Wealth Management Process.*

In our view, the 360° planning approach provides the best opportunity for implementing and maintaining a successful Family Wealth Management Plan.

360° Family Wealth Management

Kestra Financial

$88 Billion
Assets under advisement[1]

Fidelity Institutional℠

$8.8 Trillion
Total Customer Assets (AUA)[2]

Wealth Preservation

- Wealth Transfer Planning
- Asset Protection
- Wills and Trusts
- Legacy Planning
- Gifting Strategies

Advisor Coordination

- CPA
- Lawyer
- Banker
- Valuation
- Mergers & Acquisitions

Investment Management

- Personal CFO
- Asset Allocation
- Performance Reporting
- Investment Policy Statements
- Cash Flow Management

Personal Family Office

360° Family Wealth Management

Philanthropy

- Family Foundation
- Charitable Trust
- Annual Giving
- Donor Advised Funds

Risk Management

- Life insurance
- Long Term Care
- Property & Casualty
- Long Term Disability

Family Business Strategies

- Exit Planning
- Succession Strategies
- 401(k) Planning
- Key Employee Retention

360°

The 360° Six-Step Family Wealth Management Process

Step 1

Get The Facts

The first thing we do is meet with you to understand the vision for your family, the resources you have available to achieve that vision, and the potential obstacles that may stand in the way of turning that vision into a reality. As your vision unfolds, we may raise some specific tax, legal, or other financial issues that you may not be aware of, so that we can gauge your level of concern with those issues, and whether they need to be addressed as part of the overall planning process. We then begin gathering the facts along with the various pertinent documents.

Typically, this involves collecting, but may not be limited to:

- ✓ Financial Statement(s)
- ✓ Copies of wills, trusts, insurance policies
- ✓ Recent tax returns
- ✓ Investment statements
- ✓ Asset Titling
- ✓ Buy-Sell and business agreements

Once we have reviewed all relevant documents and have clarity and agreement on the ultimate objective, we can then turn our attention to our assessment of where you stand in relation to your vision and goals.

We call this next step, "*The 360° Stress Test*."

Step 2

Take The 360° Stress Test

The purpose of the 360° Stress Test is to understand the full implications of your current plan; its strengths, weaknesses, and critical issues that must be addressed immediately.

We do this by getting answers to the following questions:

- ✓ What does your will say and is it properly integrated with your overall plan?
- ✓ Is your will tax-sensitive?
- ✓ If trusts are part of your current plan, are they properly designed to maximize your Wealth Preservation and Transfer Plans?
- ✓ Is your insurance set up in a tax-wise fashion, and is it consistent with your current objectives?
- ✓ Are your investments intelligently diversified?
- ✓ Are you exposed to unnecessary taxes and other risks?
- ✓ Do you have a Buy-Sell agreement in place, and does it accurately reflect your intentions? Is it properly coordinated with your will?
- ✓ Are you adequately insulated from property or liability risks?
- ✓ Are you charitably inclined, and are you expressing this intention persuasively?
- ✓ Are you fulfilling your fiduciary responsibilities with your 401(k)?
- ✓ Are your advisors properly coordinated to achieve your family's financial goals?
- ✓ Has your wealth plan been updated to reflect life and circumstance changes?
- ✓ Do you have an Executive Retention Program in place?
- ✓ And many other questions.

Once we have fully evaluated the strengths and weaknesses of your current plan, we can begin to design a plan that addresses critical issues, weaknesses, and areas for improvement.

We call this this next step, "*The Wealth Preservation Blueprint*."

Step 3

Develop the Wealth Preservation Blueprint

In this stage, we will begin discussing the various potential strategies and plan designs that might make sense for you. Some approaches will be simple and straight forward. Others may involve some tradeoffs. Some of the tools will require little administration while others may be more complex and costly requiring more attention. During this phase, it is also essential to include other members of the planning team in the discussion and evaluation process.

Our Proprietary Financial Condition Model allows us to evaluate the full range of planning tool options, and to assess each planning technique by itself, and in conjunction with other tools. In this way, we can determine if the approach we are considering is as effective as possible in terms of costs, benefits and trade-offs.

Let's look at a possible "cost, benefit and trade-off," example that illustrates the kind of decision you may need to make as part of the blueprint. Say we are considering transferring shares of the family business to the next generation. Naturally, if we are giving away shares now, we will reduce wealth for the parents.

The Financial Condition Model will help us determine if and how the reduction in wealth may impact such factors as:

- ✓ The parent's standard of living
- ✓ Control of the business
- ✓ Overall estate tax consequences
- ✓ Wealth creation for the next generation and beyond

We can then select the best approach to transferring shares, in the most effective way possible.

Once we have considered all potential planning tool approaches, we will arrive at a final list of vetted and mutually agreed-upon strategies. This action list will become the "Wealth Preservation Blueprint," ready for implementation.

Step 4

Implementation

Now, coordinated by your 360° Wealth Manager, the professionals go to work implementing the blueprint, and addressing the six distinct but interrelated areas, as further detailed below.

Wealth Preservation

We will work closely with your attorney to draft your wills, trusts, and other legal documents. If you own a business, we will very likely create voting and non-voting shares of stock to facilitate transferring shares while retaining control of the company. A Family LLC may be created to allow for valuation discounts. Valuations for gift tax purposes will be performed

Investment Management

We will create an Investment Policy Statement that reflects your investment goals, risk tolerance and time horizon, within a suitable Asset Allocation plan. We will rebalance the existing portfolio in a tax-sensitive fashion to be more closely in line with the new Asset Allocation plan.

Once the new model is in place, you will receive simple, easy to understand monthly and quarterly performance reports. These reports will display accurate rates of return for all your investments so that you always know how you are doing. We will closely monitor the entire portfolio on an ongoing basis, rebalance as needed and manage taxes to optimize results. If required or desired, we can provide Personal CFO services to pay bills and manage your cash flow.

Risk Management

There are two aspects of wealth creation. The first is making money, and the second is not losing money. From a net worth point of view saving $1 million is the same as avoiding a $1 million loss.

→ **Property and Liability**

During the 360° Stress Test, we reviewed your exposure to property and liability risk. In conjunction with the insurance team, we will make any changes or updates to your coverage to eliminate any unnecessary vulnerabilities and potential for losses. At the same time, we will strive to obtain the optimum coverage at the most competitive rate.

→ **Long-Term Disability**

If we have determined that your ability to earn an income is essential to your overall financial health, then we will consider LTD insurance. We will design and implement the most cost-effective program to replace your earned income if you were to become disabled. Furthermore, sometimes Disability Insurance is used as part of a Buy-Out program.

→ **Life Insurance**

Replacing wealth lost to estate taxes is the number one use of Life Insurance for families of means. Life insurance can also be used for estate equalization, funding Buy-Sell Agreements and Executive Retention Programs. Once we have determined if and how Life Insurance will be part of the Plan, we will manage the underwriting and implementation process from beginning to end.

→ **Long-Term Care Vs. Self-Insuring**

Traditional Long-Term Care Insurance is recommended for people who have insufficient assets for self-insurance. Self-insurance refers to funding the expenses of long-term care through assets and other financial resources that a person owns, which is often the choice of wealthy families. Once we have determined how Long-Term Care will be a part of the overall Plan, we will manage the design and implementation of a Self-Insurance program.

Family Business Strategies

→ **Exit and Succession Plan**

Exit and Succession Planning for a family business is a complex area and requires the most coordination among advisors. As important, the Plan must have built-in flexibility to accommodate changing family dynamics and other life circumstances over time.

→ **Key Employee Retention Plan**

For some families, the long-term goal is to successfully pass the company to the next generation. For others, the next generation may not be interested in or capable of taking over and running the business, in which case, we must develop an alternative exit plan. As part of the process, we determine whether a Key Employee Retention Plan, often referred to as a "Golden Handcuffs" program, must be designed and put into place.

→ **401(k) Plan**

We review and audit the existing 401(k) plan.

Our goal is to:

- ✓ Eliminate any fiduciary liability exposures
- ✓ Improve the investment lineup
- ✓ Lower all plan expenses
- ✓ Simplify administration
- ✓ Educate the employees
- ✓ Increase participation
- ✓ Maximize owner contributions

Philanthropy Planning

Charitable giving is a very personal area. Some families make gifts each year. Others want to include a family foundation as part of the Plan. There are also opportunities to support charities while receiving significant tax benefits. A charitable giving plan can be fine-tuned to a family's specific needs and desires.

Potential strategies include:

- ✓ Family Foundation
- ✓ Charitable Trusts
- ✓ Annual Giving
- ✓ Donor-Advised Fund

Once we understand the short and long-term philanthropic desires of the family, we will design and implement the optimum giving Plan.

Advisor Coordination

There will be several professionals involved in designing, implementing and keeping your Plan on track, including:

- ✓ CPAs
- ✓ Attorneys
- ✓ Bankers
- ✓ Valuation Specialists
- ✓ Merger and Acquisition Advisors
- ✓ Insurance Advisors
- ✓ Investment Managers
- ✓ Trust Administrators

As we have previously discussed, we believe it is critical to have a 360° Wealth Manager coordinate the team of advisors working on your behalf. It can make the difference between a plan that performs as intended, and a plan that falls short.

Step 5

Review The Completed Plan

Once the plan is fully implemented, we will meet with you to review the completed plan, and to provide you with a binder that contains all the documents related to your Plan along with the names and contact numbers of your team of advisors. As an option, you can also have the entire completed plan stored on a secure cloud server for your reference.

The good news is that if and when you have any questions related to any part of the plan, you can refer to the binder, or, you can get the answers you need directly from your *360° Wealth Manager*, your single point of contact.

Step 6

Keep The Plan On Track

Step Six may be the most important step of all. It is a major milestone to have completed a fully coordinated and comprehensive *360° Family Wealth Management Plan*. At the same time, we know that most successful and wealthy family offices will experience change over time. Businesses expand and contract, real estate is bought and sold, children are born, people get married, families expand, and family dynamics alter. Furthermore, world conditions change.

A successful family wealth management plan must be flexible enough to accommodate these changes and take into account new conditions as they arise or are anticipated. This is critical to keeping a well-crafted plan on track and fully effective. Also key, is that you should expect to sit down with your full 360° Family Wealth Management Team at least once a year to review the plan and make sure that the plan still reflects your family's goals.

All changes and revisions to the plan, as they occur, will be incorporated into the Plan Binder, so that anytime you refer to the binder you will have up-to-date information.

There you have it, a complete overview of *360° Family Wealth Management*.

During the next chapters, we will delve into each of the planning areas in more detail.

Wealth Preservation

Failure to have a comprehensive 360° plan in place often leads to the demise of the family business due to family conflict and poor planning.

The Fate Of
The Family Business

INTRODUCTION

Family-owned businesses are the backbone of the American economy, and employ a substantial portion of the workforce. Some of the better-known family-owned companies are Ford, Wal-Mart, Comcast, News Corp and Mars.

PROBLEM

It is not surprising that many founders of family businesses want the fruits of their labor to survive and continue to grow for generations to come. Unfortunately, without proper planning, a business may not last through the founding generation. Why is this?

In our experience, one reason family businesses fail to continue from generation to generation is that family business leaders sometimes keep transition plans in their heads rather than commit them to a formal succession plan. Failure to have a comprehensive 360° plan in place often leads to the demise of the family business due to family conflict and poor planning.

CONCLUSION

We have a saying in our business, "You don't really get to know someone until you have probated an estate together." Unfortunately, in the absence of a clearly defined business succession plan, many families end up fighting over control and the profits from the business. In the same way that, "Good fences make for good neighbors," having a well-designed and fully implemented family business succession plan can help mitigate many of the conflicts that arise when ownership of the family business changes.

Wealth Preservation Mistakes Of The Rich and Famous The Miami Dolphins

CASE STUDY

INTRODUCTION

Most people assume that the rich and famous have a legal and financial team of advisors who are making sure that their wealth is protected for future generations. Unfortunately, this is often not the case. It is our observation that most people try to avoid dealing with anything to do with death and taxes, even though we all know that both are inevitable. While this is understandable on an emotional level, it is nevertheless of critical importance to address these issues head on rather than to procrastinate. Not having a proper Wealth Preservation and Transfer Plan in place can be devastatingly costly. Here is a real-life case study to illustrate this point:

PROBLEM

Back in the 1980s, the Robbie family owned the Miami Dolphins and the stadium they played in, the Joe Robbie Stadium. Joe Robbie died in 1990, and his wife Elizabeth died a year later. At that time, his estate was worth over $100 million, with most of the net worth represented by his ownership interest in the Miami Dolphins and Joe Robbie Stadium. When advisors calculated his estate tax bill, it was in excess of $40 million. The family was forced to sell the team and the stadium for $109 million to cover the estate tax bill owed to the IRS.

After the taxes and other expenses were paid, Robbie's seven children each received about $5.5 million from the proceeds. Of course, most people would still think that kind of money is a lot. But consider this - Wayne Huizenga, the man who purchased the team and stadium from the Robbie family in 1994, subsequently sold it to Steve Ross in 2009 for $1 billion!

If the family had developed a Wealth Preservation and Transfer plan during Joe Robbie's life to mitigate the estate taxes that would be owed at his death, they would have had the option of maintaining ownership of the team. Twenty years later, they would have realized a significantly larger payday. Unfortunately, they never had the opportunity.

CONCLUSION

It does not really matter if you are talking about a $5 million, $10 million, $100 million or a $1 billion business, many of the issues are the same. If it is important to you to preserve your valuable business and assets for future generations, then it is critical that you do significant planning BEFORE a triggering event takes place. As the famous saying goes: "***The time to put on your parachute is before you jump out of the plane.***"

Where Do You Want Your Assets To Go?

INTRODUCTION

*Upon passing, our assets will ultimately end up in
a combination of the three following areas:*

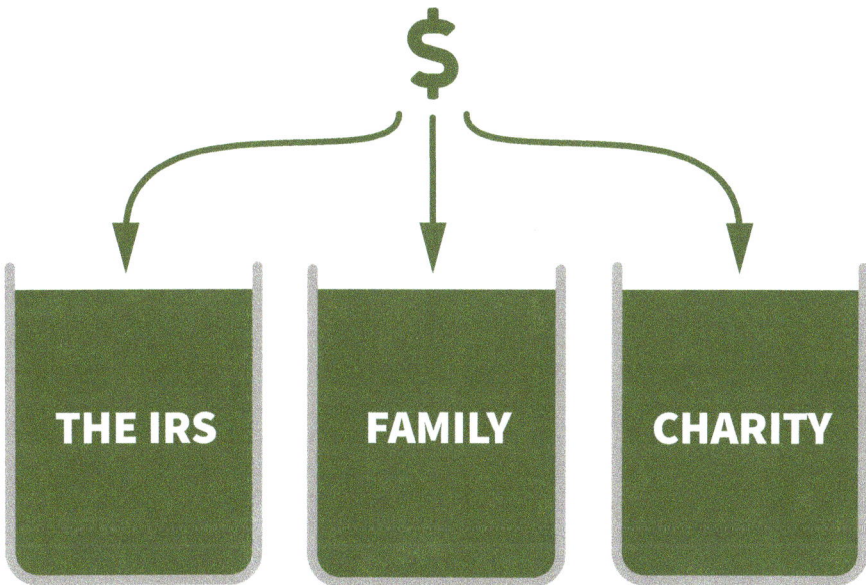

PROBLEM

We often poll the audience in our 360° Family Wealth Management seminars by asking the following question: "If you were to wave a magic wand and have the perfect wealth transfer plan designed exactly the way you want, and have your assets pass to exactly whom you want, what percentage would you want to go to each group?"

Not surprisingly, their answer most often is:

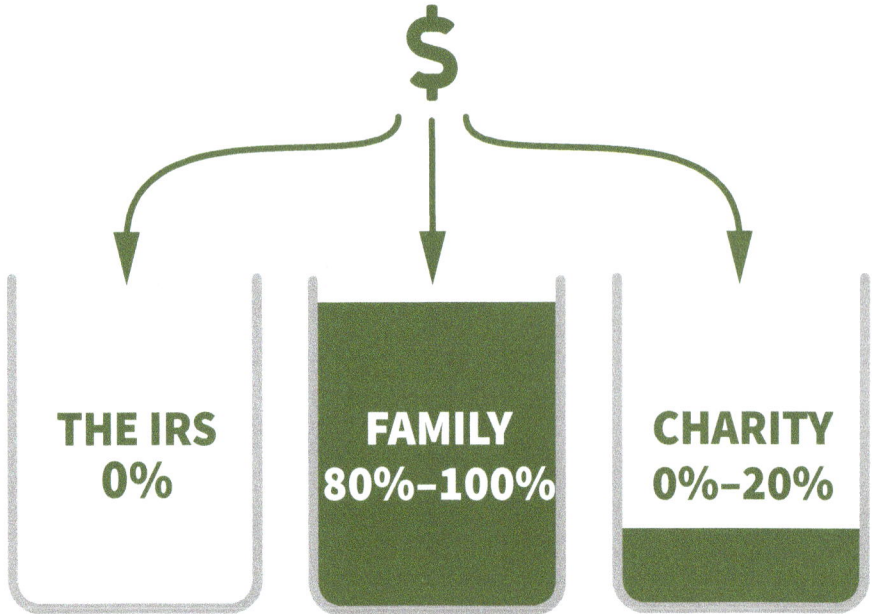

THE IRS	FAMILY	CHARITY
0%	80%–100%	0%–20%

Why?

Because most people feel that they have paid income taxes, sales taxes and property taxes their whole lives, and would rather not pay any more upon their death. They want the bulk of their wealth to go to their family, and perhaps a small amount to their favorite charities.

Almost everyone makes charitable contributions each year. This helps others in need, makes the giver feel good, and provides a charitable tax deduction. Nevertheless, for people who are charitably inclined during their lives, very few include any significant charitable giving as part of their wealth transfer plan. It is important to realize that there are many ways that charitable planning can be used, not only to benefit charities, but also to provide income for the family, foster excellent values within the family, and reduce income and estate taxes.

The problem is that without significant planning in advance, the dispersal of assets will end up looking more like this:

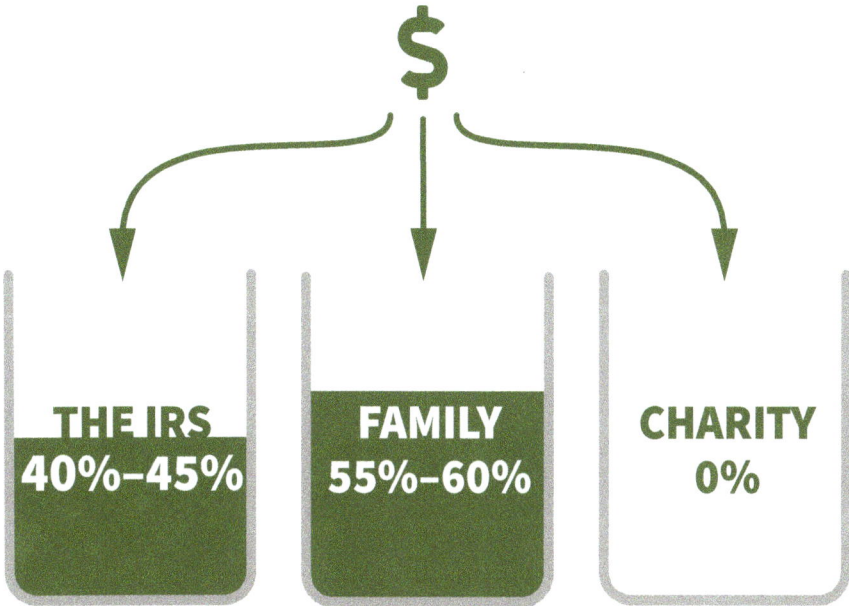

$

THE IRS
40%–45%

FAMILY
55%–60%

CHARITY
0%

Not what people generally would want!

CONCLUSION

If you have strong ideas about how and to whom your wealth should pass, now is the time to undertake significant planning, IN ADVANCE, while you can. Otherwise, the IRS could end up with up to 45% of your estate, your family could be shortchanged, and charities important to you will be excluded. The good news is that through a skillful use of wealth transfer planning techniques and tools, you CAN accomplish what you want.

Federal & State Estate Taxes

As you can see, one of the biggest obstacles preventing you from transferring your wealth to your family and favorite charities is taxes: Federal estate taxes, and, depending on where you live, State estate taxes. As onerous as these taxes can be, it is possible to minimize or eliminate their wealth-destroying effects, but only if you take well-crafted actions in advance. Before we get to some of these strategies, let's look at these specific taxes.

FEDERAL ESTATE TAXES

Federal estate tax laws have gone through a major transformation over the past two decades and have been at the center of major political wrangling. Not long ago, every taxpayer was allowed to leave $600,000 to the next generation without federal estate tax. For a brief time in 2010, the federal estate tax was actually zero. The most famous person to benefit from that year's tax law was George Steinbrenner. His death seemed perfectly timed to minimize estate taxes. It was reported that his heirs potentially saved over $600 million in estate taxes. Unfortunately, subsequent legislators have made a variety of deals that brought back the estate tax, although not at a level as onerous as it once was.

Currently, in 2021, individual taxpayers may leave a total of $11,700,000 to their heirs without estate tax. Any amount over $11,700,000 would be taxed at a maximum rate of 40%. This means that in 2021, a couple can each leave $11,700,000 to their heirs for a total of $23,400,000. Effectively, less than 1% of all US families will ultimately owe federal estate taxes. However, for those families with estates of significant value, putting a plan in place to address estate taxes is crucial.

2021 Federal Estate Tax Law	
Maximum Exemption Amount	$11,700,000
Combined with Spouse	$23,400,000
Maximum Marginal Rate	40%

Another positive aspect of the current tax law is something called portability. Before this provision was added, when all assets were passed to a surviving

29

spouse, the exemption of the first spouse to die would be wasted. To take advantage of the exemption, each spouse had to have assets equal to the exemption amount in their individual names, and the will had to pass assets to a trust with special provisions to ensure the exemption would be used. Although these trusts are still beneficial, they are no longer necessary to make use of the exemption. Portability now generally allows any unused exemption from the first spouse to be used at the death of the second spouse.

This means that upon the death of either spouse, in this case, let's say the death of the husband, the wife can use her $11,700,000 exemption plus his $11,700,000 exemption (a total of $23,400,000) to pass along to their children, grandchildren and other heirs, without any federal estate tax.

STATE ESTATE TAXES

Is it necessary to create a complicated estate plan or is a basic, simple will sufficient, if a married couple's estate is under $23,400,000? If the only concern is federal estate taxes, then a simple will may be all that is needed in today's tax law climate.

Unfortunately, unlike the federal government's current treatment of estate taxes, many states feel that they can't afford to give up revenue. They have imposed stricter estate tax laws that may affect a broader section of the tax-paying public. The estate tax laws of your resident state, therefore, will need to be critically considered as part of your overall Wealth Transfer Plan. Let's look at an example of a state with high estate taxes, to illustrate our point.

NEW YORK ESTATE TAXES

New York still has an estate tax and the program is onerous. Currently, the first $5,850,000 escapes state death taxes. However, if the estate exceeds the exemption by 5% or more, the tax goes back to dollar one, effectively eliminating the benefit of any exemption. The maximum marginal tax rate is 16%, and the effective rate on a NY estate of $10 million is almost 11%. So, while an estate of $23,400,000 million might escape federal taxation, it could be subject to a NY state tax bill of over $3 million.

CONCLUSION

Now that you know what you may be up against, we are going to examine the various tools, strategies, and pitfalls to avoid, in order to help reduce or even eliminate the detrimental effect of poor planning and estate taxes.

Why An 'I Love You Will' Is Not Enough

CASE STUDY

Don't Leave Your Assets Unprotected!

INTRODUCTION

If you are like most people, you have the most common type of will, the "I Love You Will." It says, "I leave all my assets to my beloved spouse, and upon the death of my spouse, our assets go to our lovely children." This seems straight forward and protective enough, BUT IS IT?

PROBLEM

In the previous section, we looked at the wealth-destroying effects of Estate Taxes. However, estate taxes are not the only way that the value of your estate can be endangered.

Leaving assets to the next generation in an unprotected fashion can also destroy wealth through divorce, lawsuits and bankruptcies. Suppose you have managed to accumulate an estate totaling $100 million, consisting of your homes, investments, business(es), retirement plans and life insurance. Surely, your intention is to fully protect the value of your estate for generations to come. Here are two examples of the most common, unpleasant, potential pitfalls of failing to use Asset Protection.

EXAMPLE ONE

Consider a scenario in which a spouse passes away, leaving all the assets to the surviving spouse. What would happen if the surviving spouse remarries and subsequently dies or gets divorced? Without proper planning, some or all of the family assets could end up with the new wife or husband, thereby inadvertently disinheriting the children.

EXAMPLE TWO

Consider a scenario in which your son or daughter were to get married and then, someday, get divorced? Based on our client base, we often see first marriages end up in divorce, and sometimes see second marriages fail as well. It is entirely possible that the assets you spent a lifetime accumulating could end up with your future ex-son- or daughter-in-law, or, as we say in the trade, a future "outlaw."

CONCLUSION

Most people think Asset Protection is too complicated and costly, but that is not true. Almost everyone can benefit from putting a "moat" around their assets to protect them from future "outlaws." Consider designing a will that not only maximizes asset protection, but is also Tax Sensitive, as we will discuss in the next section.

The Tax Sensitive Will Protect Your Assets

INTRODUCTION

As we have seen, the typical "I Love You" will is an ineffective wealth transfer tool. A properly designed and structured Tax Sensitive Will can take full advantage of current tax laws for the benefit of the family for generations to come, AND protect family assets from "creditors and predators." It is a critical Wealth Preservation and Transfer tool.

A Tax Sensitive Will is also known as an A/B Will or a Credit Shelter/ QTIP Trust Will, which are essentially similar will structures that are designed to:

- ✓ Provide income, and principal if needed, for the surviving spouse's lifetime.
- ✓ Build a "moat" around the assets to shelter them from the claims of creditors or future "outlaws."
- ✓ Minimize estate and gift taxes for the next and future generations.
- ✓ Shelter future trust asset growth from estate taxes.
- ✓ Provide income and principal, if needed, to future generations.

Let's look at basic examples of how a properly designed Tax Sensitive Will might work:

THE CREDIT SHELTER TRUST (CST)
PROTECTING MAXIMUM ESTATE TAX-FREE CREDITS

A Credit Shelter Trust allows a Spouse, upon passing, to leave the maximum estate tax-free credit allowed by the then current law ($11,700,000 in 2021). This trust will not only shelter the tax credit for the children but will allow the sheltered amount to be invested and to grow, ultimately providing the full value and benefit to the children, without being subject to federal estate taxes.

Bear in mind, that while the trust will grow estate-tax free, it will have to pay income taxes on any taxable earnings or capital gains.

CREDIT SHELTER TRUST
FUTURE BENEFITS

While the CST protects assets and their growth for future generations, it may also need to protect the surviving spouse. Therefore, maximum flexibility can be built into the trust so that the surviving spouse will have access to trust assets as needed, to maintain the lifestyle to which the spouse has become accustomed.

Generally, two main provisions can be built into the trust to accommodate special access to the trust funds:

- ✓ Access to income and principal at the trustee's discretion, in any amount. This means, of course, that a trustworthy trustee must be selected, who understands the family, understands finances and will cooperate with the surviving spouse.

- ✓ Limited power of appointment. This provision gives the surviving spouse, upon death, the right to give or provide more to one child than the others. No one new can be included in this provision. This feature is strictly optional and can be included, or not, depending on individual family circumstances.

Trusts can be effective asset protection tools.

THE QTIP TRUST

A QTIP Trust should be considered to protect the additional family wealth, which can be substantial. QTIP stands for Qualified Terminable Interest Property.

While there is no specific tax benefit as part of this trust, it can primarily be used as an asset protection tool that contains several important features:

- ✓ The surviving spouse **MUST** receive **ALL** the income from this trust each year. Of course, this can be somewhat controlled by the choice of investments. If limiting income is desired, for example, very low or no dividend investments can be purchased.

- ✓ The trustee can give additional principal to the surviving spouse, at his/her sole discretion. Again, as always, it is vital to have a trustee who knows the family, is knowledgeable about finances and understands the wishes of the decedent.

- ✓ The most important distinguishing feature of this trust is that when the surviving spouse eventually passes away, the remaining assets in this trust will go to the heirs of the first spouse to die.

This type of planning might be applicable to several different life circumstances. Let's discuss the two major uses:

FIRST MARRIAGES

If the surviving spouse were to remarry, there is always a chance that assets will become commingled. Examples might be the purchase of a new house that is jointly owned, jointly owned bank or investment accounts or artwork displayed in the new house. The problem arises when the surviving spouse remarries, commingles some assets with the new spouse, and then predeceases the new spouse, or gets divorced. It is entirely possible that some of the assets that were intended to pass on to the children of the first marriage could end up with the surviving spouse's future ex-husband or wife.

However remote, if you both want to ensure that the assets accumulated during your marriage go only to the children or selected heirs of that marriage, then this tool can be useful.

SECOND MARRIAGES AND BLENDED FAMILIES

Many people marry again and often create blended families consisting of "his/her" children, "my" children and sometimes, "our" children. In addition to all the previous concerns, there are now some new concerns to address.

A QTIP Trust can be used to:

✓ Ensure that the surviving spouse can continue to live in the style accustomed to, for life.

✓ Direct how individual or jointly owned assets specifically go to "his/her" or "their" children.
For example, the first spouse that dies may want to leave assets directly to his or her children from a previous marriage(s).

CONCLUSION

Everything outlined above can be written into the CST/QTIP Trusts. If desires can be put into words, they can be put into a trust, for the most part. Consider the use of trusts in any scenario where remarriage is possible, or when dealing with children from different marriages leads to a need to treat "his, hers and ours" specifically and differently.

CREDIT SHELTER/QTIP TRUST – ADDITIONAL BENEFITS
THE PASSING OF BOTH PARENTS

Let's consider what happens after both the mother and father have passed away. In most wills, the assets are either given to the children outright, or when they attain certain ages. A common arrangement is to distribute the assets one-third at age 25, one-half at 30 and the balance at 35. However, what happens if they get divorced at 40? It is entirely possible that the future "outlaw" could end up with half of "your" money. If it is important to you to keep all the assets you have accumulated in your lifetime in your bloodline, and your estate is large enough to consider a tax sensitive will, then it makes sense to include multi-generational tax reduction and asset protection tools in your will.

This means that after both you and your spouse pass away, your assets are left in trust, safeguarded for your children, FOR LIFE! The assets remain in the trust and your children would receive income and principal at the trustee's discretion. For this to work, again, your children must have a friendly trustee. You can even give your child the right to remove and replace an uncooperative trustee. In many cases, one sibling can be the trustee for the other, essentially creating a mutual, cooperation pact. The concept here is that we are protecting the assets FOR your children not FROM them.

In addition, most people don't realize that almost anything you can buy outside a trust, you can buy inside a trust. The purchase of investments, a house, a car, other real estate, or even starting a business, can all be done within the protective trust structure. What is the advantage of doing this? It shields your assets by building a "moat" around them. No one unintended, can get to those assets. If your child is sued, goes bankrupt, owes taxes or gets divorced, no one and no court (barring unusual circumstances) will be able to cross that moat and storm the castle to attach the assets in the trust. At the same time, your children can freely use the assets through the cooperation of their friendly trustee.

> *With poor or no planning your assets could pass on to a surviving spouse's ex-husband or wife instead of your children.*

GRANDCHILDREN, THE THIRD GENERATION

Looking farther into the future, let's consider what happens when your children pass away. Imagine that you left $10 million in the Credit Shelter Trust for your daughter. She is a wise steward and spends or invests the income from the trust each year but allows the principal to grow. Suppose she lives another thirty years after you die.

Our hypothetical trust has now grown to $40 million during that time. When your daughter leaves those assets to your grandchildren, there will be no estate tax! Hopefully, your grandchildren will also be smart stewards of money and their estate will continue to grow, protected from estate taxes. They will enjoy the same benefits as your children did. They will have access to income and principal as necessary, while continuing to have the same asset protection moat around their money.

CONCLUSION

Compare the above results of the Tax Sensitive Will to the typical "I Love You" will. You decide that the trust business is just too complicated and just leave your daughter the $10 million outright, in her own name. She is still a good money manager and spends and invests the income in exactly the same way. When she dies, she leaves her now $40 million estate to her children, your grandchildren. Without the trust structure, the $40 million estate becomes taxable, and any amount in excess of her lifetime exemption (currently $11,700,000) will be taxed at 40% Federal and possibly up to 16% at the state level, depending on where she lives. The value of her estate could theoretically be reduced by half!

These are not leading edge, aggressive strategies. These are basic, tried-and-true strategies that can provide your hard-earned assets both asset and tax protection, for *generations to come*.

A QTIP Trust protects your assets for your children, not from them

Estate Equalization

Does My Wealth Transfer Plan Treat My Children Equally?

INTRODUCTION

One of the most common and thorny problems we encounter with family businesses, is that there are often children in the business and children out of the business. Most parents want to treat their children as fairly as possible. The challenge is that the family business often represents the major part of the family assets, and unless the plan is to liquidate the business, it can become a challenge to provide an equal amount of assets to each child.

Further complicating this problem, is that depending on how the assets are bequeathed in the will, estate taxes can have a major impact on any remaining liquid assets. It is therefore critical to engage in advanced wealth transfer planning, to anticipate the issues that may arise.

PROBLEM

Mr. and Mrs. Smith met with us to discuss their wealth transfer plan. They have three children, a son and two daughters.

Their total net worth is $100 million, comprised of the following assets:

Assets	
Primary Residence	$ 5,000,000
Vacation Residence	$ 2,000,000
Savings & Investments	$ 45,000,000
Qualified Plans & IRAs	$ 8,000,000
Business Real Estate	$ 15,000,000
Business Interests	$ 25,000,000
Total Estate	$100,000,000

Their thinking was that they would leave the business and the business real estate totaling $40 million in value to their son. He had started working summers in the family business when he was a teenager, and after college, he joined the business full time. Over the years, he had been instrumental in growing the business, and proven capable of taking over and running the whole show when the time came. They figured they would split everything else between their two daughters, about $30 million for each daughter. It wasn't exactly equal, but they felt that their son had made such a major contribution to the growth of the business that he should get a little extra.

There was only one problem. They forgot about their favorite relative, Uncle Sam! The way their existing will was drafted, it essentially bequeathed the business and the business real estate to their son, and provided for their daughters to split the "residuary" estate. That is a fancy way of saying that the daughters would split what was left over.

Unfortunately, unless the will states otherwise, the law says that after direct bequests are made, any estate taxes due must be paid BEFORE the balance of the estate, or the residuary, is dispersed. Based on their will, the son would have received assets worth $40 million, as they intended. However, the $60 million balance of the estate was subject to federal and state estate taxes in the amount of $30 million. This left the daughters with $15 million each, definitely NOT what the parents had intended.

Estate Equalization Failure

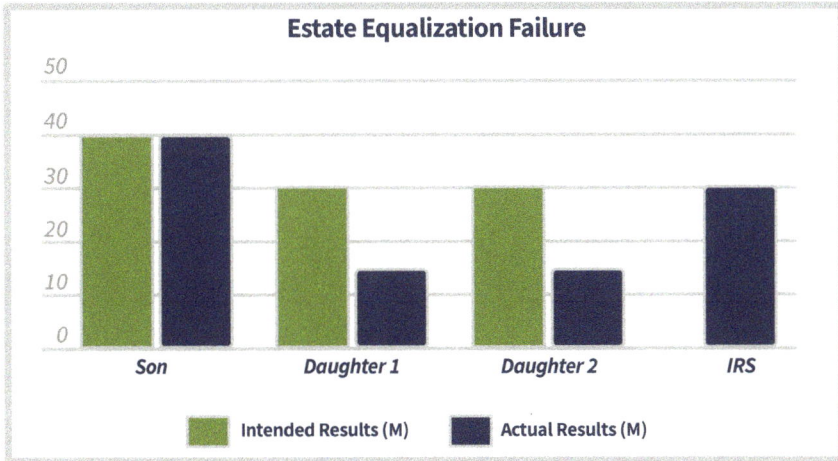

CONCLUSION

Had we not stepped in and incorporated estate planning tools into their will and their wealth transfer plan, the parents would not have realized their intentions, and would have inadvertently caused relations between their children to be strained, not the family legacy they intended. If you have children in the business and children out of the business, you need to consider engaging in significant wealth transfer planning, to ensure that you preserve your wealth for the next generation and that your desires are met.

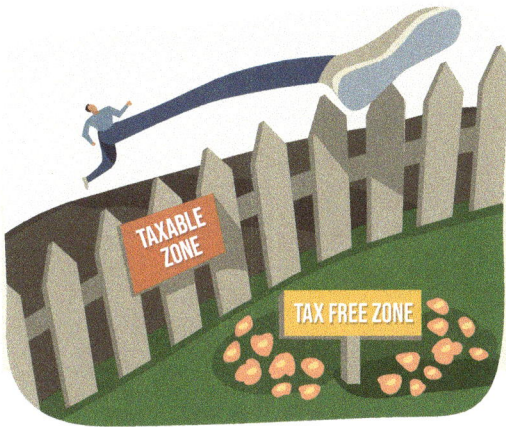

Wealth Transfer Planning Tools – Benefits of Hopping the Tax Fence

INTRODUCTION

After a lifetime of paying income taxes, no one wants to then pay an additional tax at their death. The good news is that there are ways to move your estate out of the reach of the IRS and into a tax-sheltered environment. In layman's terms we call this "Hopping the Tax Fence." Imagine you are standing on one side of a hurricane fence. We are going to call this side of the fence your "Taxable Zone." Everything on the other side of the fence we'll call your "Tax-free Zone."

OBJECTIVE

Our overall planning objective is to legally minimize your estate taxes, maximize asset protection, and pass more of your wealth to your heirs consistent with your Multi-Generational Wealth Building Goals.

TAXABLE ZONE

Here is how things work in the Taxable Zone. Everything you leave to your heirs is subject to federal and state estate taxes up to almost half of your estate. (This will vary depending on where you live). If you leave your assets outright to your heirs, those assets could potentially be exposed, not only to estate taxes, but to the claims of divorcing spouses, creditors or bankruptcy courts.

When your children, in turn, leave those assets to their children, your grandchildren, the assets will be taxed again. The very same assets that you accumulated over a lifetime, that were already reduced by lifetime income taxes, and 40 - 50% estate taxes at your death, will AGAIN be taxed at roughly another 40-50% at the passing of your children. In addition, those assets will still be without any protection in the event of a divorce or creditor action.

You can see that the Taxable Zone is not a very nice place to leave your assets. Who wouldn't want to hop over the tax fence and park their money on the other side, in the Tax-Free Zone? One can and one should!

TAX-FREE ZONE

Every American can employ the tools to maximize their Tax-Free Estate, but most don't know how to use these tax-free tools to maximum advantage. Let's examine these tools in more detail.

ESTATE TAX PLANNING TOOLS

There are three major planning tools that are part of the tax code in 2021 that can help you to "Hop the Tax Fence." Through the skillful use of these tools, families may be able to significantly reduce their tax exposure. The tools are:

The tools are:

	Single	Joint
Annual Exclusions	$15,000	$30,000
Lifetime Exemptions	$11,700,000	$23,400,000
Multi-Generational Exemptions	$11,700,000	$23,400,000

As you will see, each of these tools involves some form of giving money away.

ANNUAL EXCLUSIONS

Each year, a taxpayer can give away $15,000 to anyone they want to without incurring any gift tax. A married couple can double this amount and give away $30,000 a year. These amounts are indexed for inflation. As a practical matter, most families will use this exclusion to give money to their immediate family, including siblings, children, grandchildren, nieces and nephews.

This is a "use it or lose it" tool. This means that it can only be used once per year and cannot be carried over from one year to the next. In addition to money, almost anything of value can be given, including stocks, bonds, mutual funds, and even shares of a business or real estate.

Gifts can be made directly to heirs or into certain kinds of trusts for future use. This aspect of gifting can be tailored to each family's unique situation, and can even be different for each family member, as the individual financial situations dictate.

FEDERAL EXEMPTIONS IN 2021

As of 2021, a taxpayer is allowed pass up to $11,700,000 at death to the next generation, and a married couple can pass up to $23,400,000, without incurring federal estate taxes. You may also make gifts up to these limits at any point in your lifetime without incurring estate or gift taxes. Any amount above these numbers would be subject to tax of up to 40%. Again, gifts can include cash, stocks, bonds, mutual funds, real estate or shares of the family business.

MULTI-GENERATIONAL EXEMPTION

If a family situation warrants it and it is desired, an estate can be structured to allow the Lifetime Exemptions to pass along tax-free to the grandchildren.

CONCLUSION

These three major planning tools provide a significant Wealth Transfer opportunity to move cash, investments or other assets to your heirs on a tax-favored basis. The next aspect of "Hopping the Tax Fence" that needs serious consideration is whether to give these assets outright or in trust.

> *Use a Wealth Preservation Trust to Hop the Tax Fence.*

Wealth Transfer Planning Tools
Outright or in Trust?

The most important aspect to consider, when using these tools, is whether to give the assets outright to your heirs or in a trust designed to maximize asset protection and wealth preservation. For the purposes of this discussion, we will call this a "Wealth Preservation Trust." Leaving your assets in a Wealth Preservation Trust is like building a moat around your money. In most cases, if drafted correctly, it would be almost impossible for anyone, other than the people you have authorized, to get to that money.

Here are some scenarios to illustrate this point:

- ✓ If one of your children marries and then subsequently divorces, the future ex- spouse will not be able to get to the money that is in the trust.

- ✓ If one of your kids gets involved in a lawsuit and loses, the money in the trust will be protected.

- ✓ If your son or daughter declares bankruptcy, neither the court nor their creditors will have a claim on the trust assets.

- ✓ When your children ultimately pass away and leave the assets in this trust to their children, there will be no estate tax. The assets will still enjoy the same asset protection.

Depending on the state where the trust is set up, it is possible for this trust to continue in perpetuity, with the same protections.

There is a common misconception that trusts are intended to keep heirs from getting to their inheritance. Some advisors will set up a trust to deliberately trickle out the money each year. In our opinion, there are better and more family-friendly ways to set up a family trust. Unless there is a specific problem in the family, like a spendthrift child or a special needs child, we generally design the Wealth Preservation Trust to protect the assets FOR the heirs not FROM the heirs.

One of the best ways to do this is to appoint a "friendly" trustee and give that trustee broad powers. You can also give the trust beneficiary, your child, the right to replace the trustee with someone who is more "friendly." One of the most common arrangements is to have siblings be the trustees for each other. In this way, they can cooperate and protect each other at the same time.

Take advantage of Annual Exclusions using a Wealth Preservation Trust.

BENEFITS OF HOPPING THE TAX FENCE
USING ANNUAL EXCLUSIONS

We have previously discussed the importance of taking advantage of Federal Tax Exemptions within a Wealth Preservation Trust, in order to "Hop the Tax Fence."

Let's look at some scenarios that highlight the benefits of taking advantage of Annual Exclusions using a Wealth Preservation Trust:

→ Your son and his wife have several young children and are getting ready to buy their first house. You and your spouse could give them $30,000 each year, tax free, to help them with the expenses.

→ Your daughter works in the family business and hopes to someday take over the business. You want to gradually transfer some ownership of the business to her, and you do this via a Wealth Preservation Trust. Imagine that you give her the allowable tax-free amount of $30,000 in company stock every year for 30 years, and that the company grows at 5% a year. Upon your passing, your daughter would receive approximately $2,000,000, estate and gift tax-free. Once the gift is made, all future growth of that gift is considered "out of the Taxable Zone" and in the Tax-Free Zone!

→ Mr. and Mrs. Smith are both 55 years old. Their estate is worth $120 million. They decide to give away $30,000 to each of their three children and two grandchildren every year, using their Annual Exclusions, for a total of $150,000 annually, and put the gifts into a Wealth Preservation Trust. Each year, for 30 years, they invest in a variety of mutual funds and exchange traded funds and earn, on average, 6% per year. They both pass away at age 85. Based on this scenario, the children and the grandchildren would share almost $12,000,000 in their Wealth Preservation Trust, completely estate tax-free.

→ In contrast, let's imagine that Mr. and Mrs. Smith skipped the trust idea because they thought it was too much trouble. Instead, they established a separate brokerage account in their own names and invested the $150,000, each year, in the exact same funds. In their will, they specified that the money should be split among the children and grandchildren. Upon their passing, this account would have been part of their overall taxable estate. Before their heirs could receive the funds, they would first have had to pay approximately $5 million of estate taxes, leaving a balance of only $7 million to be split five ways.

CONCLUSION

Clearly, the benefits of "Hopping the Tax Fence" using a Wealth Preservation Trust are convincing and compelling! Keep in mind, as we say in the business, "Don't try this alone at home." Designing a Wealth Preservation Trust can be complicated and requires expertise. In addition, there are important annual administrative tasks that must be performed to protect the tax-free status of the assets in the trust, all of which can be overseen by your 360° Wealth Manager.

Levels of Wealth Transfer Planning

INTRODUCTION

How much Wealth Transfer Planning is enough? We have developed a Pyramid depicting the progressive levels of Wealth Transfer Planning to help you decide which tools might be appropriate for your particular family situation.

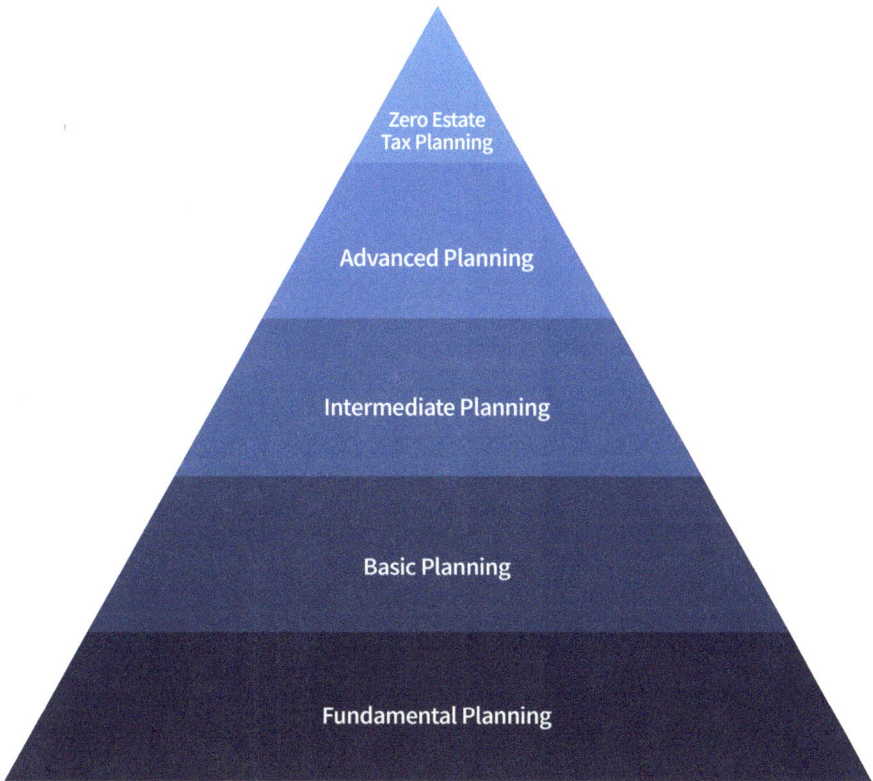

Zero Estate
Tax Planning

Advanced Planning

Intermediate Planning

Basic Planning

Fundamental Planning

FUNDAMENTAL PLANNING

Anyone who has a spouse, children and/or assets of any significance needs Fundamental Planning.

This includes:

- ✓ Designing proper Wills
- ✓ Making full use of Credit Shelter Trusts
- ✓ Setting up Durable Powers of Attorney
- ✓ Completing Living Wills and Health Care Proxies
- ✓ Funding Survivor Needs
- ✓ Using an Irrevocable Life Insurance Trust to own any Life Insurance
- ✓ Setting up a Buy-Sell Agreement if Partners are in the business
- ✓ Making sure that Asset Titling is coordinated with Wills and Buy-sell Agreements
- ✓ Utilizing a Golden Handcuffs Plan if you have key executives

BASIC PLANNING

Once your total estate reaches the $10 - $20 million level, it is time to start thinking about Basic Planning.

In addition to the items listed under Fundamental Planning, you need to include:

- ✓ Creating and funding a Wealth Preservation Trust.
- ✓ Making gifts into this trust using the Annual Gift Tax Exclusions.
- ✓ Creating a tax-free fund to help offset any costs associated with settling your estate.

INTERMEDIATE PLANNING

As your estate grows past the $20 million level it is time to think about putting the following additional techniques into action:

- ✓ Consider giving away some or all of your Lifetime Credit during your life instead of waiting until you pass away.
- ✓ Explore the use of valuation discounts as part of your gifting program if you own a business or investment property.

✓ Use your Generation Skipping Exemption to designate assets to go to your grandchildren without estate taxes.

ADVANCED PLANNING

If you have effectively used all of the Intermediate Planning techniques and you still have a potential tax exposure, you may want to consider using these tools:

✓ Consider using an Estate Freeze to lock in the value of your estate at today's value and transfer all the growth of your estate from the "Taxable Zone" to the "Tax-Free Zone."

✓ Establish specialized trusts to leverage your gifts by increasing their tax-free value to your heirs.

✓ Sell highly appreciating assets to a trust for the benefit of future generations instead of giving away assets.

ZERO-ESTATE TAX PLANNING

Some people don't want to pay any estate taxes. This is possible utilizing charitable trusts and/or a family foundation in conjunction with the three planning tools: Annual Exclusion Gifts, Lifetime Credits and Generation Skipping Exemptions. In implementing a zero-estate tax plan:

Consider implementing a Charitable Remainder Trust which:

✓ Provides a lifetime income, leaving all the trust assets to your favorite charity when you pass away and, if desired,

✓ Also provides some replacement income from those assets for your heirs.

Consider establishing a charitable family foundation legacy, that can be administered by your heirs.

CONCLUSION

Your specific situation, including your net worth and objectives, will ultimately determine how high on the pyramid you climb. Here again, the devil is in the details, do not try this alone at home.

Investment Management

*The secret to success is not timing the market but **TIME IN THE MARKET***

Strategies To Help Maximize Your Money

DOES ACTIVE MONEY MANAGEMENT WORK?

It is almost impossible for anyone to beat the market for any prolonged length of time. We conducted in-depth research into the factors associated with investment management including expenses, turnover, tax efficiency, beta, alpha, standard deviation, risk levels and style drift. We then compared our results with other professional money managers, and each money manager's results with their relevant benchmark, and to their peer group.

What did we discover? The majority of active money managers could not beat, let alone meet their benchmark, and a great many under-performed their peer group. An S&P Dow Jones 2019 Indices Report found that: "Over long-term horizons, 80 percent or more of active managers across all categories underperformed their respective benchmarks."*

Active Fund Managers Trail the S&P 500 For the Ninth Year In A Row In Triumph For Indexing – 3/15/2019 – CNBC.com.

We concluded that active money management does not work well enough, long enough, or consistently enough to justify paying for it, except in very few instances.

CAN YOU TIME THE MARKET?

Over the years, some of our clients have requested that we attempt to time the market. In our opinion, to time the market successfully and consistently, an investor must make two correct timing calls: 1) Sell near the top of the market, and 2) Buy back in at or near the bottom of the market.

This is completely counter intuitive for many people. We have seen investors get caught up in the excitement of bull markets and want to buy more, while market bottoms tend to make them afraid of investing, fearing that things could get much worse.

The real problem with timing the market is that often the market moves higher in short bursts of activity and growth. Many studies have shown that if you miss just a handful of these high growth days in the market, your returns can really suffer. We don't believe market timing is a good strategy, but we do like to buy quality investments when they are on sale.

To this day, when the market swoons, we see opportunity.

LANDSCAPING PROVIDES A TERRIFIC METAPHOR FOR INVESTING

When you plant young trees you must have patience, as it will take them years to grow and mature enough to provide the kind of privacy, protection and beauty you originally envisioned. Along the way, they will experience and withstand storms that may down some branches, so they will require trimming from time to time, and, of course, they will need the regular nurturing of water and sunlight.

Tending to an investment portfolio is like the caring and nurturing of trees. Over time, the market will experience good and bad years. However, history has shown that over the long haul, stocks will average about 10% growth per year. At that rate, a three-foot baby tree will grow to be a six-foot tree in roughly seven years and so on.

Investment portfolios, like trees, need patience, tending, and time to develop and grow. Still, many people feel the pull and allure of what is almost an impossible thing to do, and that is, trying to time the market.

Stock market growth occurs in bursts. It does not happen in tiny bits of growth every day. If you happen to miss the few growth spurts that occur during the up periods, then your long-term average will go way down. It is like saying, "Every time there is a storm, I will pull up my trees, store them in the garage and replant them when the storm is over." Surely you recognize that this would stunt the growth of your trees, just as it would your investment portfolio. With respect to the stock market, we believe that: The secret to success is not timing the market but *TIME IN THE MARKET*.

CAN WE PREDICT THE FUTURE?

The other ability that timing the market requires is the ability to predict the future. Some of the smartest, best educated people on the planet are employed in the financial community attempting to predict the future; the future of interest rates, the economy, the election, the various crises across the world, the inflation rate, the actions of the fed, the public's reactions to the state of affairs, and the weather.

It is our opinion that almost none of them get it right. We have all had the experience of watching TV and hearing a famous economist predict a recovery, and five minutes later listening to an equally well-qualified economist predicting a recession. Nobody knows, and no one can predict the future. If people really could predict the future, why would they share this knowledge with the public? Why not just trade on their special insight and become "gazillionaires?" If they felt charitable, they could set up a foundation and become world famous philanthropists.

To quote a much used adage: "Prediction is very difficult, especially about the future." In our opinion, predicting the future, and timing the market, do not work for us mere mortals.

When the market swoons, we see opportunity.

INFORMATION IS NO LONGER THAT UNIQUE

Technology has changed the way the entire asset management business operates. There was a time when information gave you a true advantage. In the days of sailing ships, an alert merchant might notice a shortage of a particular commodity in London and dispatch his purchasing agent on the fastest ship he could hire, to buy a ship load of that commodity from another country, and bring it back to London to sell at the higher prices brought about by the shortage. Sooner or later the other merchants would catch up and the shortage and the attendant opportunity for high profits would disappear.

Before computers, there existed an "old boy network" of school chums who would share what was really inside information. This allowed those in the group to profit handsomely. For most of history, the "big, smart money" would be presented with private investing opportunities that the average investor did not even know existed. In our opinion, even today, it may be true that institutional inves-tors have a pricing advantage over the average retail investor, but the informa-tional advantage is rapidly disappearing.

Today, everybody has access to information 24/7/365. If anyone really has an informational advantage, in other words, true inside information, it is prob-ably illegal to act upon it. How can anybody find out something truly special and unique about Microsoft, Intel, GE, GM, IBM, Apple, Exxon or Facebook? The smartest people on the planet are constantly scrutinizing every aspect about these firms, and many of them are making their insights available to the public. Information is no longer that unique.

Investment portfolios, like saplings, need patience, tending, and time to develop and grow.

SO, WHAT DO WE DO?

If it is difficult or impossible to beat the market, then we believe the next best plan is to **capture the market**. As we pointed out earlier, we have observed that the average money manager cannot consistently meet or beat their benchmark or their peer group, and the average investor seriously lags the overall mar-ket. Our conclusion is that delivering market returns is actually a merit-worthy achievement.

HOW DO WE DO IT?

First, Own The Market

We want to own the market. We do this in our core portfolio, which is a wrap account, by investing in a fully diversified global strategy that is customized for each client's specific goals, risk tolerance and time horizon. We invest in large, mid-size and small companies from large, medium and small countries. Naturally, we invest in the big household names such as IBM, ExxonMobil, Pfizer, Apple and GE, but we also include smaller companies where there are potentially greater growth opportunities.

We invest globally because the US only represents about half of all the companies in the world. Many of the smaller countries offer potentially great opportunities because they are growing fast to try and catch up with the rest of the world and give their citizens all the benefits of a modern society. We balance our selection between fast growing companies, and more mature, typically stable companies paying dividends. Of course, diversification does not guarantee a profit or protect against a loss and dividends are not guaranteed. In addition, investing in smaller, international and faster-growing companies may entail greater risk than in their larger, more established counterparts.

As global market conditions change, we make modest strategic changes to keep pace with the overall economic picture. This constitutes our Core Portfolio where we try to capture the overall global market. We know that no matter what happens, we strive to position ourselves to keep pace with the market. In our opinion, keeping pace with the market, as we mentioned already, is something a great number of active money managers do not consistently achieve.

Second, Use Exchange Traded Funds (ETFs)

One of the investment tools we use, when building client portfolios, is Exchange Traded Funds (ETFs), for many reasons.

→ ETFs can offer the individual investor the ability to buy a portfolio of securities like stocks, bonds, currencies or commodities in one simple package. These funds have been around for twenty years or so, and are one of the fastest-growing investment vehicles available today. Historically, most ETFs were index funds and were priced throughout the day like a stock. When the first ETFs were created, there were only a few options available. The "Diamonds" were a fund consisting of all 30 Dow Jones Industrial Average stocks. The "Spyders" were a fund that held all 500 stocks that make up the S&P 500. Today, there are thousands of ETFs, giving investors the opportunity to invest in just about any slice of the global financial world. For example, you can buy an ETF that owns only health care stocks, gold, euros, or just companies that do business in China.

→ ETFs can be bought or sold any time during the trading day, unlike open-ended mutual funds and unit investment trusts that only trade once a day. This gives investors the chance to place limit orders, sell them short, or trade based on the market moves during the day, if that fits into an investor's trading strategy.

→ Generally, most index funds are designed to have a low expense ratio, typically ranging between .08% and .70%, compared to average mutual fund expenses, that can range between 1.50% and 2.00%. In addition, ETFs can be very tax efficient. To fulfill liquidation requests, a mutual fund manager may have to sell assets that could generate a capital gain. This capital gain is then passed on to all existing shareholders who must pay taxes on these gains even though they may not have sold any of the shares they own in their Portfolio. On the other hand, when you invest in ETFs, you will only pay taxes on capital gains that you may incur when you sell shares in your Portfolio at a profit. Please keep in mind that you still may have to pay a commission charge to your broker for purchasing or selling ETFs.

→ ETFs lend themselves to effective tax management. Currently, if you sell an asset at a loss and buy it back within 31 days, the IRS will not allow you to write the loss off, as it violates the wash sale rule. ETFs are sufficiently varied to allow you to harvest losses, while following this rule.

→ ETFs are fully transparent, meaning you can go online anytime 24/7/365 and see exactly which securities you own at that moment.

→ ETFs can be used as part of a passive investment strategy. Research from the CNN Money website supports the concept that overall investment strategy or asset allocation can contribute much more to your long-term investment results than individual stock selection. For example, it may be more important to be in the energy sector when energy is growing rapidly than trying to pick the best energy stock.

Based on research and our many years of experience, we have built our portfolio strategies using ETFs for stock, bond, commodity, currency and real estate exposure. In certain situations, we also use individual bonds. Instead of spending our time and resources on fundamental stock research, we focus on attempting to identify long-term investing trends or themes. We then adjust the asset allocation to reflect our viewpoint and tactically rebalance the allocation several times during the year. Using this approach, we have helped our clients meet their financial goals and objectives

We should point out, however, that there are drawbacks to investing in a passive, ETF strategy. A well-designed, passive strategy could deliver the overall market return. By contrast, an active money management strategy might occasionally outperform the overall market. As with any passive or active money management strategy, there are risks associated with sector investing. You could make an investment in a sector that declines in value. You might also pick a sector that performs well but neglect to sell it at an opportune time. While ETFs present the opportunity for a flexible investment strategy, they may not be suitable for some investors.

As investment managers, one of our bedrock beliefs is to focus on the elements we **can** control, and not worry too much about things that we **cannot** control.

What Are Some of The Areas Where We Have Little Or No Control?

- ✓ The weather
- ✓ World politics
- ✓ The actions of the Fed
- ✓ Interest rates
- ✓ Inflation
- ✓ The election (beyond our own vote)
- ✓ Monetary and fiscal policy
- ✓ The day to day movement of the stock market

> *Focus on the elements we **can** control.*

Instead, Let's Look At Some Of The Things We Can Control:

EXPENSES

We are on a constant crusade to drive down every cost associated with investing. As the old adage wisely says: "A penny saved is a penny earned."

TAX MANAGEMENT

We don't want to spend one more dollar in taxes than necessary. Towards the end of each calendar year, we scrutinize every account for opportunities to reduce taxes. We do this with a combination of tax-loss harvesting, charitable giving, tax deductions, tax deferrals and tax-advantaged investments.

CASH MANAGEMENT

We encourage our clients to steadily and regularly add to their portfolios and contribute to their retirement plans. While we never try to put our clients on a budget, we do promote sensible spending and close monitoring of cash flow to help avoid future problems.

ASSET ALLOCATION

We strive to craft intelligently designed portfolios that take full advantage of Modern Portfolio Theory and advances in Behavioral Finance. We work to match the investor's Risk Tolerance, Time Horizon and Financial goals to their portfolio allocation. We maintain a long-term outlook and try to avoid getting "spooked" by the day to day gyrations of the markets. Asset allocation does not protect against loss of principal.

Maintain a long-term outlook and try to avoid getting "spooked" by the day-to-day changes in the market.

PORTFOLIO REBALANCING

Periodically, we rebalance portfolios, bringing them back to their original, intended allocation. This means taking profits by selling some of the winners and using that money to buy some other good quality funds when they are temporarily out of favor. We call this, "selling high and buying low at the margins." Please keep in mind that rebalancing assets may involve selling assets in a taxable account, and can, therefore, have tax consequences on any gain resulting from the sale, which is why it is important to consult a professional tax advisor.

RISK REDUCTION

→ **Company Risk:**
Where possible, we attempt to reduce the risks that are somewhat within our control. The first is company risk. The extreme case of this is the corporate executive who has all of his or her financial net worth in the stock of the company where he or she works. Is there some overwhelmingly compelling reason to take this kind of risk? If not, consider becoming more diversified.

→ **Market Risk:**
By now, you know we think it is dangerous to attempt to predict the short-term moves of any market. Protect yourself by blending together several different types of assets. We call this diversification.

Over the years, we have had many new clients come in with what they thought was a truly diversified portfolio. One gentleman came in quite distraught. He had over 40 different funds from five different companies using eight different advisors. Even though he was drowning in a sea of paper each month, he believed he was protected because he had so many different brains helping him invest. However, when we analyzed his portfolio, we discovered that of the 40 funds, 37 of them were the same types of funds. None of his advisors had talked to each other, and so ended up duplicating each other's efforts. When the market tanked, his investment funds had all tanked together.

→ **Currency, Political and Interest Rate Risk:**
By using a globally diversified strategy, we not only attempt to reduce market risk, but also help reduce currency, political and interest rate risk. The portfolios we create and manage for our clients may include large-, mid- and small-sized US companies, and comparable International companies from developed and emerging countries. They could include growth companies, value companies, and/or sector strategies. The fixed income portion could include government bonds, municipal bonds, corporate bonds, high-yield bonds, short-term bonds, international government bonds, emerging market bonds and some cash. To diversify even further, we may include REITs and annuities.

What Else Can We Control?

SERVICE AND REPORTING

As your 360° Wealth Managers, we communicate with you on a regular basis. We review portfolio performance, provide recommendations, rebalance and update portfolios as needed, and attend to your cash flow requirements. Just as important, we coordinate the other members of your wealth management team to ensure that your changing circumstances and needs are addressed on an immediate and timely basis, and are accurately updated and reflected in your Wealth Transfer and Management Plan.

Our professionals take care of all reporting and paperwork. We provide you with a secure, online portal so that you can access your accounts 24/7/365, and see how your portfolio is doing at any point in time.

Risk Management

Life insurance plays a critical role in Wealth Preservation, Business Succession and Wealth Transfer Plans.

Life Insurance — The 'Unloved' But Effective Wealth Preservation and Wealth Transfer Tool

INTRODUCTION

Life insurance tends to be a rather unloved financial tool because it basically pays off in the event of death. It really should be called death insurance, but then, no one would ever buy it because, understandably, nobody really likes to talk about death. As a result, most people give little thought to how their life insurance program is set up and whether it is structured to take full advantage of the unique tax benefits that the IRS bestows upon life insurance and life insurance only. In particular, life insurance plays an important role in wealth preservation, business succession and wealth transfer plans. It can provide funds to offset the bite of estate taxes and can also provide funding to facilitate a business succession plan.

Whole Life, Universal Life, Variable Life and all other types of "permanent" insurance have three main components:

- ✓ A Premium
- ✓ A Death Benefit
- ✓ A Cash Value

If set up correctly, the cash value can grow without tax, and in certain circumstances, be withdrawn without tax. This potential feature of life insurance policies is as a result of current IRS regulations. However, one of the most common and costly mistakes is for people to apply for life insurance and then set it up in such a way as to make the death benefit estate taxable. This can be a serious and expensive error, especially since, with a few simple precautions, the entire life insurance death benefit can be received by the beneficiaries both income and estate tax free!

Most people are unaware that the IRS considers life insurance an asset that can be owned.

Generally, there are three parties to a life insurance contract:

→ **The Insured**
This is the person whose death triggers payment of the death benefit.

→ **The Beneficiary**
This is the person who will receive the proceeds
of the policy when the insured dies.

→ **The Owner**
This is the person who owns the policy, is responsible for making
premium payments, can make withdrawals from the cash value
and, most importantly, can select or change the beneficiary.

When someone with significant assets passes away, his or her executor, CPA or attorney will tally up the assets to determine if any estate taxes are owed. The asset calculation may include homes, businesses, other real estate, cash, stocks, bonds, mutual funds, IRAs, other assets, such as paintings, jewelry and cars, and any **life insurace** owned by the deceased.

Let's look at two common examples to illustrate the potential problem of not setting up life insurance properly.

EXAMPLE 1- WIFE IS THE BENEFICIARY

A family has a net worth of approximately $100 million. As part of their wealth transfer plan, the husband buys $35 million worth of life insurance. He names his wife as beneficiary so that upon his passing, she has access to the proceeds.

The true purpose of the life insurance is to fund the federal estate tax, the state estate tax, and income taxes that will be due at the second death. When the husband dies, the insurance pays off and goes directly to his wife, as planned. The wife invests the $35 million, and only withdraws the income and dividends it yields, keeping the principal intact.

The wife received the insurance proceeds both income and estate tax free. However, when the wife ultimately passes away, that $35 million will be added to her total assets for estate tax calculation purposes. Her heirs will now owe approximately $14 million in estate taxes on the $35 million insurance proceeds - assets that could have been tax free.

EXAMPLE 2 - CHILDREN ARE THE BENEFICIARIES

A family has a net worth of approximately $100 million. As part of their wealth transfer plan, the husband and wife buy $35 million worth of second-to-die life insurance. They maintain control of the policy as owners and name their children as beneficiaries. Their intent is that the insurance proceeds will help their children by offsetting the bite of federal estate taxes, state estate taxes and income taxes. The husband passes away and later, the wife passes away. The insurance pays off and goes directly to the children.

Though the money from the insurance company went directly to the children, because the parents owned the policy, the IRS treats it as if they bequeathed the death benefit to the children. As a result, the insurance proceeds of $35 million are added to the family's estate assets for tax calculation purposes, and the heirs now owe an additional $14 million in estate taxes. This tax could have been completely and legally avoided with one simple tool –*The Life Insurance Trust.*

THE LIFE INSURANCE TRUST

You may hear it called a Wealth Preservation Trust or a Family Trust. This trust functions in several critical ways. First and most importantly, if structured properly, it will shelter the life insurance proceeds from taxes. In the examples above, the entire $35 million could have been received by the heirs, income and estate tax free - a savings of approximately $14 million. The set up and design of this kind of trust, however, requires that certain steps be followed diligently for this tool to work.

As soon as a decision is made to include life insurance as part of a family wealth transfer plan, arrangements must be made to create a Life Insurance Trust, as follows:

✓ An attorney would draft a document creating a trust to be the owner and beneficiary of the life insurance.

✓ The trust would have its own tax ID number and file a tax return.

✓ A trustee would be named to administer the trust. The trustee should not only understand how to handle money but be familiar with the family. values and dynamics. The trustee does not have to be a professional. Many people choose a close family member or trusted friend.

✓ The trust document would contain complete instructions telling the trustee what to do with the assets. Within certain guidelines, these can be as liberal or strict as desired.

✓ In many, if not most cases, the provisions of the Life Insurance Trust would mirror the trusts under the will, so that all the concepts that apply to setting up a trust as part of the will would apply here.

✓ An important feature accomplished by this type of trust would be the creation of a "moat" around the assets. This would protect the assets from future divorcing spouses ("outlaws") and other creditors.

✓ This trust can be designed to continue far into the future. If your kids do not spend all the money in the trust, they can pass what is left along to the grandchildren, and, if desired, **generations thereafter, with NO tax liability.**

✓ Once the trust drafting process is initiated, the life insurance process may start.

✓ It generally takes 6 to 8 weeks to complete the insurance underwriting process, providing ample time for the trust to be finalized and signed

✓ The trust must be executed before the final insurance applications are signed. The trust, as the owner and beneficiary since inception, receives the insurance proceeds free of income and estate taxes.

CONCLUSION
AFTER THE LIFE INSURANCE TRUST HAS BEEN SET UP

We like to say, don't try this alone at home. There are several critical administrative steps that must be followed in order to protect a trust's tax-free status.

They include but may not be limited to the following:

- ✓ The trust must be signed before the final insurance application is signed.

- ✓ A separate trust account must be set up.

- ✓ Each year, gifts need to be made to the trust for the premiums.

- ✓ Each time a gift is made to the trust, a "Crummey" letter (named after the Crummey family who first set up this kind of trust, were challenged in IRS Tax court, and won!) must be issued. The Crummey letter qualifies the gift for the annual exclusion gift treatment described earlier.

- ✓ The Crummey letter basically says, "Dear son/daughter, I am making a gift to this trust for your benefit. You have 30 days to decide if you want to take this gift out for your own use. If you decide to leave the money in this trust, then you forfeit your right to withdraw it and the trust can use these funds for other trust purposes, like paying for life insurance."

- ✓ Finally, all premium payments must come directly from the trust account.

As you can see, a Life Insurance Trust is a critical wealth preservation and transfer tool, as it can basically take an entire life insurance policy out of the taxable estate. In our example, when both husband and wife have passed away, the entire $35 million death benefit would be received by the trust, free of any federal estate tax, state estate tax or income taxes.

Family Business Strategies
Exit and Succession Planning

Without a properly designed Buy-Sell Agreement, you may face disastrous consequences.

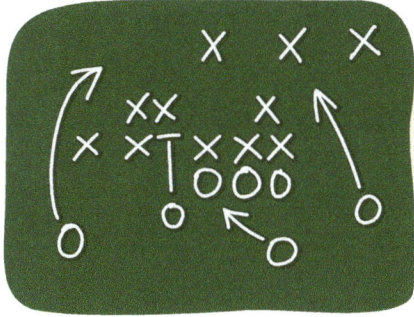

Family Business Strategies

INTRODUCTION

As we review Family Business Strategies, we will start with a series of case studies emphasizing the pitfalls of poor business exit and succession planning.

- ✓ Giving up shares of the business without giving up control
- ✓ An incomplete plan does not work
- ✓ Buy-Sell Agreement Contingencies
- ✓ Poor business succession planning
- ✓ The importance of retaining key executives
- ✓ The Golden Handcuffs Program

We then delve more deeply into the Buy-Sell Agreement, a critical exit and business succession planning tool. In fact, the heart of an exit and business succession plan is the Buy-Sell Agreement. Without a properly designed Buy-Sell Agreement you may face disastrous consequences.

The Heir Not So Apparent — Giving Up Shares Without Giving Up Control

CASE STUDY

INTRODUCTION

A gentleman in his early 60s came into the office to meet with us. A review of his assets indicated that he owned 10% of the business he had been working in his whole adult life. As this represented a substantial portion of his overall net worth, he wanted to be sure it was protected and handled properly in his wealth management plan.

We explained that it is very difficult to dispose of a minority share in a business without the consent of the majority shareholder. It turned out, to our great wonder and amazement, that the majority shareholder was his 101-year-old father! We suggested that the best course of action would be to set up a meeting with his father to review the overall family business succession plan.

PROBLEM

They both came in to see us the following week. Dad was in astonishingly good shape for a centenarian. At one point, the son stepped out of the meeting. This gave us the opportunity to ask Dad why he had not transferred the entire business to his son yet. After all, his son had been working in the business for 40 years. More importantly, we pointed out that it would be far more costly, from a tax perspective, to pass the business on via his will than to gift a major portion of the business to his son while the dad was alive. What do you think the dad's answer was? "Since my wife died, I have been living with my son for the past few years. I am up and ready to go by 6:30 am. He isn't set to leave for work until well after 8:00 am. I just don't think he is ready and as fully committed as I want him to be, to take on more responsibility."

CONCLUSION

We explained, to his surprise, that with proper wealth transfer planning, he could:

- ✓ Give up shares without giving up control.
- ✓ Avoid leaving his son with a multi-million-dollar tax bill, by transferring the majority of his shares to his son now.

An Incomplete Plan Does Not Work

INTRODUCTION

A business owner came in to see us clearly very agitated. He and his brother owned a construction company. He had been Mr. Outside, working in the field, supervising all the jobs. His brother had been Mr. Inside, overseeing the marketing and administration of the business. This arrangement had worked well for them. They accomplished what they needed to accomplish by staying out of each other's hair, and so the business had been thriving.

Their lawyer had correctly advised them to enter into a detailed Buy-Sell agreement that would spell out exactly what would happen if one of them were to pass away or leave the business. He also advised them to obtain life insurance to finance the buy-out if one of them were to die prematurely, and to have the insurance death benefit paid to the attorney as escrow agent.

PROBLEM

Although they had taken their attorney's advice with respect to the insurance, they had neglected to make signing the Buy-Sell Agreement a priority, a draft of which had been sitting on Mr. Inside's desk for several months. Mr. Inside had passed away suddenly from a heart attack, and the Buy-Sell agreement remained unsigned. Several dire complications arose.

First, the insurance company paid the death benefit to the attorney as escrow agent. However, he could not disburse the funds to Mr. Outside because there was no agreement with instructions for him to carry out. The money was languishing in the escrow account.

Next, the family members wanted to know what was going to happen. Mr. Inside's widow expected to receive her deceased husband's salary so that she would have money to live on, even though she was not working in the business.

Mr. Inside and Mr. Outside had children in the business. The children hoped to someday step into their respective father's shoes and run the business. They also had expansion plans that they wanted to consider implementing, but it was unclear how to proceed. Who would be in charge? Who would be the eventual owners?

The business was declining because not only did Mr. Outside now have to do his AND his brother's job, but his family was being torn apart by conflict over the business and money. His sister-in-law was stressing him out, his children, nephews and nieces were pestering him daily about what was going to happen, and his lawyer was sitting on the insurance proceeds.

CONCLUSION

Mr. Inside and Mr. Outside were on the "one-yard line," with the insurance in place, and a draft of an agreement. But, because the Buy-Sell Agreement was never executed, chaos ensued. It took years of lost revenue and significant legal fees before the business succession plan was resolved. The fallout from incomplete planning also left several family members permanently estranged.

I Didn't Quit, You Fired Me!

CASE STUDY

INTRODUCTION

A father, his son and his daughter had been in business together for many years. One day, the father and son had a big argument over how the business should be run and the son walked out.

A week later, the son walked in and wanted to know where his paycheck was. His dad told him, "You quit, you are not getting paid!" The son responded, "I didn't quit, you fired me, and I want to be paid or bought out. My share is $12,500,000!" His dad countered, "What, are you crazy! Your share is not worth more than $2,500,000."

PROBLEM

Shortly after this altercation, the father came into our office with his wife and requested our help. Not only had he not spoken to his son since their altercation, but his wife was deeply upset over the family turmoil.

The good news was they had a Buy-Sell Agreement, and it was even signed. The bad news was that it was two pages long. The first page dealt with what would happen if one of the three owners were to die prematurely, the second page contained all the signatures. Nowhere was there any mention of what would happen in the event of a disagreement. The Buy-Sell Agreement was essentially useless because there was nothing in the agreement that addressed the current situation.

CONCLUSION

The family ended up in court, fighting for several years. They spent over $1,000,000 in legal fees, finally settling with the son for $12,000,000. The whole process not only hurt the family business, but more disturbing, it tore the family apart. A properly designed and comprehensive Buy-Sell Agreement would have allowed the family to successfully resolve their differences, move forward and remain together.

Dad, You Are Fired!

CASE STUDY

INTRODUCTION

Mom and Dad were partners in a car dealership. They had recently divorced but were still friends, and so had decided to continue running the business together, along with their son. They also decided that as part of their wealth transfer and business succession plan, they would give enough shares to their son so that the three of them would end up equal partners, each owning one third of the business.

A few years ago, we were playing golf at an auto industry outing with the dad. He told us that he had just "gotten back into business with a new dealership." The obvious question we couldn't help but ask was, "What happened to your old dealership?"

PROBLEM

He arrived at his original dealership one day and proceeded to do his usual walk around. He didn't like how the cars on the lot were laid out for display, so he instructed some of his staff to start rearranging the cars more to his liking. His son came out as the cars were being moved around, and they had the following exchange:

"Hey Dad, what are you doing? I just had the staff spend hours setting up the cars for display, according to my new plan."

"Well son, this arrangement looks terrible and will never work - I am fixing it.

"Dad, Mom and I just had a board meeting. We are tired of you refusing to consider new ways and approaches to this business. We can't work with you anymore. I'm sorry dad, but we took a vote and...you're fired!"

CONCLUSION

Mom and her son had two thirds of the business, a majority, and so they were able to fire Dad. There was nothing Dad could do about it. While this was not what anyone had originally intended, this was the result of poor business succession planning, and Dad got the raw end of the deal.

Make Sure Your Key Executives Don't Leave When You Need Them Most

CASE STUDY

INTRODUCTION

Joe Smith had built a prosperous business over a 45-year working career and was now ready to cash out and enjoy his Golden Years. He looked forward to playing golf, fishing and watching the grass grow in Florida. Joe hired a business broker to help him find a suitable buyer.

One of the elements that made his company so successful was that Joe had been highly effective at finding, training and developing key executives. In fact, a key selling point was that Sam and Mike, his two senior executives, would work closely with the new owner, not only to maintain the smooth running of the business during the transition phase, but to stay and help grow the business.

After several months of meetings and negotiations, Joe had a firm offer and a letter of intent to sell his business. He would soon be on his way to his dream retirement.

PROBLEM

Joe did not share his plans to sell the business with Sam and Mike. When they became aware of Joe's plans, late in the process, they felt compelled to explore other opportunities. They had been instrumental in building and operating Joe's company and had strong relationships with many of the firm's major clients. They had no ownership position in the business, no guarantee of their future financial security or financial incentive, no loyalty to the soon-to-be-new owner, and no non-compete restrictions.

They decided to take several of Joe's major accounts with them and start a new company.

When the new owner learned that Sam and Mike were leaving and taking a significant amount of the business with them, the company was obviously no longer attractive, and he withdrew his offer.

Rather than retiring to Florida, Joe now found himself back at the reins of a company that was considerably less valuable and attractive to potential buyers. Not only did he find it difficult to maintain and run his business without his two key lieutenants, he now had to fend off strong competition from them. Instead of cashing out, he faced many more years of hard work to get the company back to a profitable, "sale ready" position.

CONCLUSION

This catastrophe could have been avoided with basic planning in advance, and the use of a program to recruit, reward and retain key executives. We discuss the elements of this program in the next section.

The Golden Handcuffs Program

PURPOSE

The purpose of a Golden Handcuffs Program is to help recruit, reward and retain key executives. Rather than make them owners or partners in the business, the golden handcuffs program offers a substantial reward to key executives for performing at a high level for many years.

AGREEMENT

The heart of a "Golden Handcuffs" program is a written agreement between the company and the executive stipulating that a certain dollar amount will be contributed to a long-term savings plan. A well-designed plan spells out all the details of the plan, including the obligations of the executive and the company, the contribution, the vesting schedule, the benefit payout and the funding vehicle.

COMPANY AND EXECUTIVE OBLIGATIONS

The company is obligated to protect the executive from being fired without cause. The executive is obligated to a non-compete clause in the event the executive leaves.

CONTRIBUTION

Most plans call for a contribution of 10 to 30 percent of the executive's salary each year, for as long as the plan is in effect.

VESTING SCHEDULE

Almost every plan uses a vesting schedule. The schedule specifies how long the executive has to stay with the company before receiving the benefits. It can be for a set period of years or until an established retirement age. It can be customized for each executive, as appropriate.

BENEFIT PAYOUT

The secret to a successful Golden Handcuffs Program is to offer a significant benefit, so that executives think long and hard before accepting an offer from a competitor or deciding to leave to start their own business. A large annual contribution, coupled with a long career, can often result in a sizeable retirement benefit (potentially many millions of dollars) depending on the time frame.

FUNDING VEHICLE

The plan becomes credible to employees when they see that the company is putting money away for them. In order to comply with the relevant laws, it is critical that the funding be "informal." This means that the company can use bonds, stocks, mutual funds, annuities or life insurance in order to build up a fund that will ultimately be used to pay the executives their benefits. These funds are an asset of the company. If the executive leaves before the full vesting period, all or a portion of the benefits may be forfeited and remain an asset of the company.

CONCLUSION

A Golden Handcuffs Program is a valuable tool to lock in key executives in a wealth preservation, wealth transfer, business succession and/or exit plan. An outside buyer of your business often wants to retain management to facilitate the transition and beyond.

If family members are going to take over the business, they may need the key executives to support them while they grow into their positions. In many cases, it makes sense to "lock in" your key executives to ensure the continued smooth operation of the business.

Improperly Designed or No Buy-Sell Agreement

INTRODUCTION

While the cornerstone of a wealth preservation and transfer plan is a properly designed and coordinated will, the heart of an exit and business succession plan is the Buy-Sell Agreement. Without a properly designed Buy-Sell Agreement you may face disastrous consequences.

PROBLEM

Unfortunately, many business owners have a poorly designed agreement, if they have any agreement at all.

Without a properly designed Buy-Sell Agreement that specifically addresses the critical issues, you may be exposed to several, potentially disastrous consequences, such as:

- ✓ You could end up being partners with your deceased partner's spouse. Furthermore, chances are good that your deceased partner's spouse will be a non-working partner. You could end up doing your share of the work AND your former partner's share of the work for half the benefit.

- ✓ Conversely, if you were to pass away first, your spouse could become dependent on the good graces of your partner.

- ✓ Most certainly, you could be involved in long, protracted, expensive and unnecessary legal battles.

- ✓ Very possibly, you could be exposed to high and unnecessary taxes.

- ✓ Lastly, your own preferred plans as to how you want to pass along the business may be disrupted and unfulfilled.

All these situations would undoubtedly prevent you from being able to continue to give your full focus and attention to running and growing your business.

CONCLUSION

Most business owners agree that in the event of their passing, they would want to ensure that their businesses continue. When business owners contemplate setting up a Buy-Sell Agreement, they usually think about what will happen if one of the owners were to die unexpectedly. We call this a triggering event.

If one of the owners dies, the agreement would be activated and go into effect. This is usually the first but, unfortunately, the only event that most agreements address. This may be because death is final. However, there are many additional, equally significant events that, while subject to interpretation and difference of opinion, could also result in severe consequences. In our next chapter, we address: Buy-Sell Agreements — What Should They Cover?

Buy-Sell Agreements
What Should They Cover?

A properly designed Buy-Sell Agreement should address all the major events that could disrupt a business and trigger a change in the ownership structure.

Generally, an agreement should address and spell out exactly what will happen to the ownership of the business in the event of:

- ✓ Death
- ✓ Disability
- ✓ Retirement
- ✓ Divorce
- ✓ Bankruptcy
- ✓ Disagreement between partners

DEATH OF A SHAREHOLDER

The first and most obvious triggering event is the death of a shareholder. Unlike any of the other triggering events, there is no room for interpretation with death. The agreement must spell out who is going to buy the deceased partner's share, what the price will be and how it will be paid. Often, there will be some combination of lump sum and installment payments. In many cases, there will be life insurance to help provide funding for the buyout, and the agreement will specify how the insurance payments will be applied.

In many family-owned or closely held businesses the desires of the owners can change over time. This is one of the major reasons that it is vital that the exit and business succession plan be reviewed periodically to make sure it still reflects the desires of the owners. Here is a typical example:

DEATH OF A SHAREHOLDER – IN THE EARLY YEARS

Two brothers or two friends start a business as equal partners. Each partner has a family with young children. They draft an agreement and decide that if one of them were to die prematurely, the surviving partner would buy the deceased partner's share of the business. In this way, the surviving partner ends up with the business and the deceased partner's spouse ends up with the security of a cash payment. This arrangement carries an added benefit. The surviving partner avoids becoming partners with the deceased partner's spouse.

DEATH OF A SHAREHOLDER – MANY YEARS LATER

Let's say the business thrives and grows over twenty years. Owner A now has a daughter who has graduated college, joined the business and shows the inclination and ability to someday run all or part of the business. It occurs to Owner A that if something were to happen to him, under the current Buy-Sell Agreement, his partner, Owner B, would buy his family out and his daughter could quite possibly be forced out of the business. Owner A now wants to revise the terms of the agreement to allow his daughter to inherit or buy his share of the business. He also must address providing an income for his spouse.

There are many approaches to accomplish this goal. One approach might be to have a revised Agreement that provides the daughter with the ability to buy her father's share of the business. She may be able to use the ongoing profits from the business to make the payments, which would also serve to provide retirement income for her father, or survivor income for her mother. In this scenario, the daughter would be the owner and beneficiary of any life insurance funding. If death were the triggering event, the proceeds could help fund some or all of the purchase price for her share of the business.

DISABILITY OF A SHAREHOLDER

What would happen if Owner B has a car accident and is temporarily or permanently disabled? In many ways, this is a far more complicated problem than death.

First, most agreements do not mention how disability should be handled. Second, there is a lot of room for interpretation with disability. In some cases, an accident or illness might keep someone out of work for a while. When they recover, they may come back to work, part or full time. But what happens while they recover? Are they on full salary, perks and benefits? Does Owner A have to pay for a temporary replacement or just pick up the slack? It is one thing if Owner B is out for weeks or months, but what if he is out for years? At what point does temporary become permanent? Who makes the determination if a disability is full, partial, temporary or permanent?

Clearly, a disability issue in a business situation is a sticky problem. Of course, the agreement must address all of the issues mentioned above. In many cases, it is very helpful to purchase disability insurance to fund all or part of the replacement income and to resolve disability determination issues. In addition, many businesses will buy group or individual disability income policies for all or some of their employees. A disability income replacement policy can replace a portion of the disabled owner's salary while he is disabled. This reduces the burden of paying a non-productive executive while he is out on disability.

Most people are not aware that it is possible to purchase Disability Buy-Out insurance. If it turns out that a partner is permanently disabled, the policy will pay out a combination of lump sum and regular payments to help fund the buy-out agreement.

Of course, no one likes to pay insurance premiums and these premiums are not inexpensive. Yet, it often makes sense to purchase some limited coverage for one very important reason. It shifts the burden of determining if a disability actually exists to the insurance company and eliminates it as a potential point of contention between partners and their families. Essentially, the agreement says that the insurance company will make the determination if an owner is disabled. If they do, then the terms of the agreement are triggered, and all parties must abide by them.

RETIREMENT

One of the most common scenarios that most business partners encounter is the desire of one of the owners to retire before the other. Within a Buy-Sell Agreement, death or disability events usually trigger a mandatory offer and sale provision in which one owner (or his heirs) must sell and the other owner(s) must buy. The provisions relating to retirement, however, need to address some additional circumstances.

Let's revisit Owner A and Owner B, who are healthy and have lived to a ripe old age. Like many people, Owner B eventually wants to retire or simply be bought out. This may be fine, unless the business is experiencing a downturn in profits. If buying and selling were mandatory, the first person to trigger the buyout could force the other to buy them out of a failing business.

Even if the business is doing well, the first person to retire could potentially draw a large portion of the cash and profits from the business, possibly negatively impacting working capital. Owner A must now come up with the cash to pay off Owner B, and chances are good that Owner A may also have to find and hire a replacement executive, further squeezing the business cash flow. Certainly, most people would want to avoid being forced into such a situation.

Complicating matters more, unlike death and disability, retirement is not an insurable event. Many factors must therefore be addressed when designing and establishing the retirement buyout provisions. Considerations may include but not be limited to the size of the down payments, payment timelines, business valuation and the ability to sell shares to a third party.

DIVORCE

What could happen if Owner B gets divorced? Current statistics show about 50% of marriages end in divorce, so this is a contingency that should be considered very seriously. Suppose Owner B gets divorced and, in the process, the judge awards his ex-spouse 50% of his ownership share of the business. In short order, Owner A could find himself partners with both Owner B and B's estranged ex-spouse!

It is possible and advisable to include a provision that stipulates the triggering of a buy-out in the event shares are awarded to an ex-spouse in a divorce settlement. The purpose of this provision is to ensure that the ex-spouse has no ability to ever become an owner of the business, and also serves as a deterrent to even requesting the shares. Based on this provision, if the divorce court awards the soon to be ex-spouse 50% of the business, the spouse would be automatically bought out under the terms of the agreement.

BANKRUPTCY

A similar situation arises if, say, Owner B were to file for personal bankruptcy. The bankruptcy court might attach the shares of the company as part of a settlement. Again, this is an important contingency to be considered and addressed. A provision can be inserted into the agreement whereby an owner filing for personal bankruptcy triggers a buyout. As a result, Owner B's personal creditors do not end up with shares in the business.

DISAGREEMENT BETWEEN OWNERS

Envision a scenario where no one dies, becomes disabled, retires, gets divorced, or goes bankrupt. What if Owner A and Owner B start to grow in different directions? What if they develop different ideas about how to grow the business into the future and realize that the partnership should end, and they should both move on? This is a very common occurrence and, again, must be covered in the agreement. There are several ways to address this contingency. For example, this could be treated in similar fashion to a retirement situation where one partner buys out the other. Still, like all the triggering events discussed here, in addition to the details already outlined, additional details will need to be addressed in the agreement, such as the splitting up of customers, staff, equipment, etc.

CONCLUSION

A properly designed Buy-Sell Agreement should address all the events discussed in this chapter. A well-crafted agreement will clearly lay out solutions so that as life circumstances change or arise, conflict among partners (and their families) can be avoided or mitigated. The next chapter reviews types of Buy-Sell Agreements.

> *Without proper planning, an owner could end up being partners with his or her business partner's estranged ex-spouse.*

Types Of Buy-Sell Agreements

INTRODUCTION

There are three major types of Buy-Sell Agreements, each with distinct advantages and disadvantages:

- ✓ Stock Redemption
- ✓ Cross Purchase
- ✓ Hybrid or Wait and See

STOCK REDEMPTION AGREEMENT

The Stock Redemption format is the most common form of Buy-Sell agreement. The agreement is between the Company and the Individual Owners. It basically says that if a triggering event occurs, the Company will buy, and the Individual Owner involved will sell, his shares back to the Company.

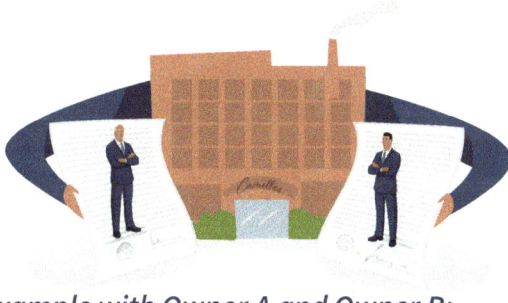

Let's use an example with Owner A and Owner B:

Owners A and B have entered into a Buy-Sell Agreement with the Company. It spells out exactly what will happen in the event one of the triggering events occurs. They have purchased life insurance, disability income and disability buyout insurance. The Company is the owner and beneficiary of the life and disability buyout insurance and pays the premiums. In this example Owner A passes away.

What would happen next?

- ✓ This event triggers a buyout under the Agreement.
- ✓ The insurance proceeds are paid to the Company.
- ✓ The Company buys Owner A's shares from his family.
- ✓ Owner B becomes a 100% owner of the business.

This type of Agreement accomplishes the desired result. The same concept and basic design would apply if there were two, five or ten owners.

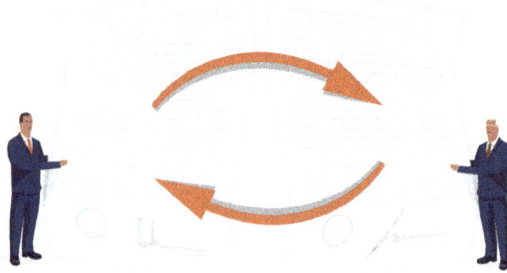

CROSS PURCHASE AGREEMENT

A common alternative to the Stock Redemption design is called a Cross Purchase Agreement. Here, the agreement is between the owners themselves, not the company. If Owner A were to pass away or otherwise trigger a buyout under the agreement, Owner B would personally buy out Owner A. Down the line, this minor difference can have major tax benefits. Here is how it would work:

Owner A and B enter into a Buy-Sell agreement with each other, NOT the company. It spells out exactly what will transpire if one of the contingency events is triggered. They have purchased life insurance, disability income and disability buyout insurance.

However, there is a big difference from the Stock Redemption design. Owner A is the owner, and beneficiary of any insurance on Owner B, and pays the premiums personally. Owner B is the owner, beneficiary of any insurance on Owner A, and pays the premiums personally. These two features give this format the name Cross Purchase. Owner A passes away.

What would happen next?

✓ A buyout under the Agreement is triggered.

✓ The insurance proceeds are paid to Owner B as Owner A's beneficiary.

✓ Owner B buys Owner A's share of the business with the insurance proceeds from Owner A's family.

✓ Owner B becomes a 100% owner of the business.

So far, the result from both types of agreements is the same. In a two-partner company, there is not much difference in setting up or administering either type of plan.

But, what if there are six partners? The Cross Purchase design would require 30 life insurance policies and if disability insurance is involved another 30! There is a solution for the multiple policy problem. Similar to the Stock Redemption Agreement, an escrow agent, and not the Company can be set up as the owner and beneficiary of the policies.

EXCESS TAXATION
STOCK REDEMPTION VS. CROSS PURCHASE AGREEMENT

Let's say that Owner A and Owner B each put up $1 million to start their business. The company is now worth $60 million, their 50% shares are worth $30 million each. Owner A passes away, and after a year, Owner B finds that he is now working way too hard and not having much fun, so he decides to sell and retire.

The real difference between the two types of agreements now comes into play.

Under a Stock Redemption plan, the following would happen:

- ✓ When Owner A dies, $30 million of life insurance would be paid to the company.

- ✓ The company would pay the $30 million to Owner A's family and the family would sell the shares back to the company.

- ✓ Owner B would then be the owner of a $60 million business that he started with $1 million, his cost basis.

- ✓ One year later, when Owner B decides to retire, he sells the business for $60 million.

- ✓ He would owe an approximately 20% capital gains tax on $59 million or $11,800,000, leaving him with $48,200,000.

UNDER A CROSS-PURCHASE PLAN:

- ✓ When Owner A dies, $30 million of life insurance is paid out to Owner B personally.

✓ Owner B pays the $30 million to Owner A's family
    in return for Owner A's 50% shares.

✓ Owner B would then be the owner of a $60 million business.

✓ One year later, Owner B decides to retire and sells the business for $60
    million. But now, his cost basis, because he personally bought out his
    partner for $30 million, is now $31,000,000 ($1 million + $30 million).

✓ Here again, he would owe approximately 20% capital gains tax, but only on
    $29,000,000 or $5,800,000, leaving him with $54,200,000. By having a tax-
    favored buyout plan, he walks away with an extra $6,000,000 in his pocket.

THE HYBRID AGREEMENT OR ("WAIT AND SEE" BUY-SELL AGREEMENT)

If it is unclear whether a Stock Redemption or Cross Purchase is the appropriate
agreement for the circumstances, or, if there is concern about changes in future
tax laws, then the "Wait and See" design is an alternative.

Here, the company is given the first right to purchase any shares available for
sale, as the result of a triggering event. If, for any reason, the corporation does
not buy any or all of the shares, then the individual owners would have the right
to buy them. If the individual owners do not buy all of the outstanding available
shares, then the company would be obligated to buy the balance of the shares.

In some cases, an escrow agent is used as the owner and beneficiary of any life
or disability insurance. The escrow agent collects the insurance proceeds and follows the purchase pattern that the company and the individual owners ultimately
settle upon.

This format provides flexibility, and may work for many Buy-Sell situations. It
should be considered if there are questions about the clear superiority of one
format over the other, and can reduce the number of policies needed in a multi-
shareholder situation.

CONCLUSION

The basic design of the Buy-Sell Agreement, the ownership and payment of
life and disability insurance, and future tax considerations must all be skillfully
designed and coordinated to achieve optimal results.

Buy-Sell Agreements
Certificate Of Value
What Is The Buyout Price?

INTRODUCTION

One of the main objectives of a buy-sell agreement is to avoid conflict, disagreement and legal battles if the agreement is triggered. We have given examples of the different scenarios that could trigger the plan, and the pros and cons of different designs. Now let's look at the biggest issue, the price. If setting the buyout price is not handled properly, the most well-crafted buy-sell agreement and best-intentioned succession plan could become derailed.

PROBLEM

Many agreements will say something like, "The purchase price will be the then current market value." But, how does one determine market price? One can well imagine that the buyer and seller may have very different opinions on the subject, so each side hires an appraiser, and now we may have conflicting valuations. Unfortunately, this can lead to conflict, disagreement, lawsuits and extended periods of time during which nothing is decided, and the business is in limbo. This is exactly what both sides hope to avoid by planning ahead.

One way to tackle this issue is to include a Certificate of Value in the original plan. The Certificate states specifically what the purchase price of the business is. The value can be based on a formal business valuation, or, the partners can mutually agree on a value. This way, there is no dispute about what the business is worth.

However, nothing in this world is static. Over time, the business will most likely evolve, and the value will change. It may increase or decrease. An effective solution to this particular concern is to meet annually and update the certificate of value either via a current, formal business valuation or by mutual consent.

If, for some reason, a year or two of updates are missed, the agreement can spell out a specific formula for adjusting the business valuation, rather than using a concept like "current market value," which is guaranteed to initiate a dispute.

An example of the basis for designing a back-up business valuation formula might be to tie the value to the most recent book value, plus or minus various adjustments.

CONCLUSION

Many circumstances can affect the value of a business. The purchase of new real estate, starting a new business, adding new partners or having children join the business are some of the more common occurrences that businesses experience over time. Meeting once a year to update the Certificate of Value affords the partners an opportunity to consider changes in the business that have taken place or are anticipated, and amend or update the buy-sell agreement.

Buy-Sell Agreements
Failure To Coordinate

CASE STUDY

INTRODUCTION

As we have discussed, many buy-sell agreements are funded with insurance. This might include life insurance, disability income insurance and/or disability buy-out insurance. It is critical that any insurance used as part of the plan be properly implemented to avoid any tax problems or unintended negative consequences. But, as we always caution, more problems are created in various planning situations by poor coordination than by poor design or poor products. This is particularly true in buy-sell planning. Here is a story to illustrate this point.

Mr. Jones had built up a profitable manufacturing business over his lifetime. As he contemplated his golden years, he realized he needed to think about a successor. He had no children in the business, but his plant manager had been with him for over 20 years and he believed this man could someday take over and run the business.

He wanted to sell his plant manager 20% of the business on very favorable terms, and to this end, had his attorney draft a Stock Redemption form of Buy-Sell agreement with the following stipulations:

- ✓ If Mr. Jones happened to die prematurely, the company would buy Mr. Jones's 80% share of the business from Mrs. Jones, and the plant manager, by virtue of being the only remaining shareholder, would transform from a 20% to a 100% owner of the business.

- ✓ Any insurance the company owned on Mr. Jones or the plant manager must be used to fund the buy-out. If, for any reason, there was no company owned insurance available, then the plant manager would purchase the business via a 10% down payment, and the balance paid out over 10 years, with interest.

✓ A Certificate of Value was signed specifying the business worth of $100 million.

✓ The purchase of an $80 million life insurance policy on Mr. Jones, and the purchase of a $20 million life insurance policy on the plant manager.

At the lawyer's suggestion, they next planned to meet with their insurance agent to obtain the necessary life insurance.

PROBLEM

When the insurance agent heard that they wanted to purchase $80 million of life insurance on Mr. Jones and $20 million on the plant manager, he set up a Cross Purchase format. This meant that Mr. Jones was the owner and beneficiary of a $20 million life insurance policy on the plant manager, and the plant manager was the owner and beneficiary of an $80 million life insurance policy on Mr. Jones.

Unfortunately, the insurance agent and the lawyer never coordinated their efforts. Mr. Jones and his family were unaware of the potential time bomb waiting to explode. You can guess what happened next.

Mr. Jones died suddenly. Mrs. Jones expected to receive $80 million in cash to support her lifestyle. But, the Stock Redemption buy-sell agreement stipulated that only company-owned life insurance was required to be used to fund the buy-out. The insurance on Mr. Jones, however, was owned by the plant manager. He correctly pointed out that he was under no obligation to use the $80 million of life insurance proceeds that he received personally, to make a lump sum payment. He was, however, obligated to pay the widow 10% of the purchase price (for the 80% balance of the business), or $8 million, as a down payment, and then to continue making payments over 10 years with interest.

Mrs. Jones was understandably very upset and took him to court, pointing out that this was clearly not the intention of the agreement. Many tens of thousands of dollars in legal fees and several years later, Mrs. Jones was forced to settle for a greatly reduced lump sum pay out.

CONCLUSION

All of this could have been avoided had the lawyer and insurance agent communicated directly to ensure that the legal agreement and the insurance set up were properly coordinated, as intended. This story also accentuates the benefit of having a 360° Family Wealth Manager overseeing and coordinating Exit and Business Succession, Wealth Preservation and Transfer Planning.

> *Due to the complexity of Buy-Sell agreements it is critical to have a 360° Wealth Manager overseeing and "conducting" the overall plan.*

Philanthropy

There are a number of different charitable giving vehicles for philanthropic intentions.

360° Family Foundation Management

INTRODUCTION

For families of significant wealth, there are a number of different charitable giving vehicles for philanthropic intentions, including Charitable Trusts, Annual Giving, Donor Advised Funds and Family Foundations. But, creating and administering these vehicles is no small undertaking, and requires significant expertise, planning, coordination and administration. Let's focus on one of the primary vehicles for families wanting to express their charitable intentions, the Family Foundation.

DEVELOP A MISSION STATEMENT FOR THE FAMILY FOUNDATION

The first step in setting up a Family Foundation, is to develop a Mission Statement. It can be as broad or specific as you want. For example, you could support the arts in general or a specific museum. You could support a particular branch of medical research, or any cause near and dear to your heart. The range of charities needing funding is full and plentiful.

You can also just leave it up to the trustees to make donations on a case by case basis.

→ **Outline An Annual Giving Plan**
It is possible to create a foundation that will live forever or only as long as an initial funding were to last. By law, a Family Foundation is required to make gifts equal to at least 5% of its total value each year. We therefore recommend that you outline an annual giving plan. This can be done in a variety of ways. You could make one large gift per year, or you may decide to make quarterly gifts to a variety of groups. You can also simply decide as you go.

→ **Select A Board Of Trustees**
You must select a board of Trustees. This is the group that will be charged with carrying out the Foundation Mission. Often, the trustees are family members and can include parents, children, and grandchildren on the Board, with the hope of passing along the founder's charitable values. In other cases, the Family prefers to have a board of professional advisors, or a combination of professional advisors and family members.

→ Develop An Investment Policy Statement (IPS)

The board is charged with managing the foundation's portfolio of assets as a "prudent person" would. In order to satisfy this requirement, it is best to follow a disciplined process that begins with determining how much risk the board is comfortable with, the time horizon for the foundation, and annual giving objectives. This process will culminate in an Investment Policy Statement. This IPS will be used by the Board to direct their investment advisors.

→ Fund The Foundation

Once the Mission Statement and IPS is in place, it is time to fund the Foundation. The Board will select the specific investment strategies, execute the documents required to set up the accounts, and then transfer the assets into these accounts.

TAKE ADVANTAGE OF TAX SAVING OPPORTUNITIES

Funding the Foundation creates two major tax saving opportunities. First, the family will receive a tax deduction when making gifts of cash, securities, real estate, or other assets to the Foundation.

Second, to achieve the most favorable tax result, it is ideal to gift highly appreciated assets. For example, if you sold a stock with large capital gains, you would first have to pay taxes on the capital gain and then make a gift of the remaining balance. On the other hand, if you gift the appreciated asset directly to the Foundation, the Foundation can keep or sell that asset, consistent with their Investment Plan. If the Foundation were to sell the appreciated asset, the Foundation would not have to pay capital gains tax, thus receiving the full value and benefit of your gift. This is one of the ways that the government supports charities.

HOLD QUARTERLY REVIEWS

As you know, the investment world is not static. Economic and market conditions are constantly changing, so it is important to monitor the portfolio on a regular basis to Keep the Plan on Track. Each quarter there should be a full portfolio performance review with the board and its advisors. One of the principal tasks is to coordinate the cash flow to meet the 5% minimum giving target, or more, if that is the board's directive. From time to time, it may be necessary to rebalance the portfolio as conditions warrant.

APPOINT A FOUNDATION ADMINISTRATOR

One or more members of the advisory team will most likely be responsible for Foundation administration. When the Foundation makes a gift to an entity, the Foundation is required to confirm that the entity has 501(c)(3) status, signifying that it is a qualified charitable entity. The Administrator will generate the checks and wires as directed by the Board. The Administrator will also issue Acknowledgement Letters to anyone making a gift to the foundation, and the donor may use this letter to document their gift for tax purposes.

Finally, and most important, the Administrator, often the CPA, will prepare the Form 990 PF, the Foundation tax return.

USE A 360° WEALTH MANAGER TO COORDINATE THE ADVISOR TEAM

Creating and administering a Family Foundation is no small undertaking. Inevitably, there will a team of advisors involved in supporting this project. Typically, an Attorney will be involved in creating the legal entity, a CPA will prepare the tax returns, the Trustees will fulfill the Foundation's Mission Statement, an Investment Advisor will manage the assets, an Administrator will carry out the Board's directives, and a team member will interact with the charities. In order for this team to be as effective as possible, it should be coordinated by your 360° Wealth Manager. This will take most of the headaches of running a Family Foundation away from you, and allow you to focus on supporting the causes that are most important to you.

Advisor Coordination

A 360° Wealth Manager conducts the overall plan to ensure that the plan is properly coordinated, kept on track, and updated as life circumstances change.

The Importance of Overseeing and Coordinating Wealth Transfer Planning Components and Advisors

INTRODUCTION

We have examined some of the major factors that, without advanced planning and proper tools, can derail wealth preservation and transfer plans. Often, each of these tools is designed and implemented by several different professionals. HOWEVER, the lack of overseeing and coordinating these individual factors, tools and professionals, can also result in unintended but severe consequences for families of wealth.

PROBLEM

We often find, when we meet with new clients, that they have some planning tools in place, but the tools are basically ineffective for one reason or another. For example, they may have a draft of a buy-sell agreement stored away in their desk drawers, but they have not actually signed the document because they have some nagging doubts about a point or two, and no one to guide them in the resolution of their concerns. In other cases, they may have a will, but it is not tax sensitive, and again, is therefore ineffective, for their purposes. Just as often, we find that provisions of their various planning tools conflict with one another, so that their intentions are not achievable.

Our new clients have lawyers, accountants, stockbrokers, insurance agents and bankers, and often, they receive good advice from these professionals in their specialized area of expertise. The problem is that rarely do they get all their advisors in one room to review all the individual planning components to make sure that everything is properly attended to and coordinated. Furthermore, seldom is there a conductor, a 360° Wealth Manager, of the overall plan to ensure that the plan is not only properly coordinated but, just as critical, being kept on track and updated as needed.

CONCLUSION

Of course, it is important to have a well-crafted will, a thoughtfully designed buy-sell agreement, a growing investment portfolio, insurance to protect your family, and financing to support your growth. However, it is critical to have a 360° Wealth Manager overseeing and "conducting" the overall plan so that all the individual elements are properly designed, implemented, coordinated, and updated as needed, to produce the desired result: Maximum wealth accumulation, preservation and successful wealth transfer.

The Passing Of Assets

INTRODUCTION

Frequently, clients come in with beautifully written wills drafted by major law firms that are not worth the paper they are written on because none of the assets pass through the actual will.

PROBLEM

A new client came into our office with five important assets including a business, a home, an IRA, life insurance and some mutual funds. However, NONE of these assets were controlled by his beautifully designed will. How could this be? When someone dies, their assets will pass in one of four ways:

→ **By Titling/Operation of Law**

In this case, the house and investment accounts were owned as Joint Tenants with Rights of Survivorship or JTWROS. In fact, the majority of family homes are owned jointly. The same is usually true of family bank accounts and many investment accounts. This means that if the husband dies, the house and bank accounts pass automatically to the wife, and if the wife dies first, they pass automatically to the husband. In this situation, however, as is often the case, our client was on his second marriage and had children from a first marriage. His case was more complicated and therefore needed a more tailored plan.

→ **By Beneficiary Designation**

IRAs, 401(k)s, and life insurance have beneficiary designations. Upon our review, we discovered that our client's will specified that he wanted to leave his IRA to his sister, a single mom supporting four kids on her own. However, his IRA beneficiary designation indicated that his IRA was to go to his wife. No matter what the will said, his wife would receive the IRA because beneficiary designations supersede wills. If this problem was not corrected, his intentions would not be met, and his sister would be out of luck.

→ **By contract**

Our new client owned a large, earth-moving contracting business with his brother. They built the business together and actually had a signed buy-sell agreement that stated that if one of them were to die, the other would buy him out. They had even purchased life insurance to help make the buy-out payment. This would have been fine, however, the complication was that the client's son had joined the business several years earlier, and it was apparent that he was very capable. Our new client dreamed of having his son carry on with the business.

Unfortunately, the lawyer who wrote the original buy-sell agreement twenty years earlier had since retired, so our client used a new attorney to write his new will, leaving the business to his son. He forgot to mention the old, out of date, buy-sell agreement with his brother. Based on that document, if he were to pass away, the business would go to his brother, not to his son. His son would have had to try to make a deal with his uncle, who, by the way, had his own son to whom he wanted to leave the business. This was certainly not what the client wanted or intended. If this situation were not corrected, the business would have passed to his brother, not to his son. Why?

Because a business contract or buy-sell agreement supersedes a will. Why? Because that's the law.

→ **By Will**

Finally, we return to the will. After beneficiary designations, titling of houses and other assets and operations of contracts, whatever is left over will be controlled by the will. In our new client's case, this amounted to just about nothing. As the situation stood, his will was ineffective. It did not address his desire and intention to protect his son or his sister.

CONCLUSION:

Even though the individual elements of a plan may be well conceived and designed, if they are not fully coordinated, the intended result may not be achieved. Unfortunately, this happens all too often. In this case, you might think it was the attorney's fault. Why didn't he ask about the rest of these elements? He probably did. In fact, he probably sent a letter to the client, after drafting the will, to emphasize the importance of coordinating the will with his asset titling, beneficiary designations and other contracts. But, in this case, the client did not understand the law or the importance of coordinating his plan, and so hired the lawyer just to draft a will.

As we discussed previously, think of your personal 360° Family Wealth Manager as someone who performs the job of architect and general contractor to develop a detailed plan, and to then supervise and coordinate the work of the various subcontractors. We believe this is the best approach to ensuring that your plan will be carried out per your intentions.

Clearly, someone with expertise must be in charge to:

- ✓ Design a well thought out, coordinated, multi-faceted plan
- ✓ Coordinate the implementation of all the individual components
- ✓ Ensure that the plan is kept up-to-date and remains on track as circumstances change

Pulling It All Together

Hypothetical 360° Family Wealth Management Case Study

CASE STUDY

INTRODUCTION

Mr. and Mrs. Smith have worked hard to build a thriving business over the last 30 years and have accumulated an estate in excess of $100 million. They are now in their mid-60s and are naturally concerned about planning for the future. They want to know if a wealth preservation and transfer plan can be designed to meet their objectives while also addressing their concerns. As our hypothetical case study shows, our answer is YES.

They have the following objectives:

- ✓ Preserve and grow their assets for their children and grandchildren
- ✓ Minimize estate taxes

They have the following concerns:

- ✓ Maintain control of the family business
- ✓ Maintain the lifestyle of the family

Mr. and Mrs. Smith have the following assets as of 2021:

Business:	$70,000,000
Business Real Estate:	$15,000,000
Personal Real Estate:	$5,000,000
Investment Portfolio:	$10,000,000
Total Assets:	$100,000,000

PROBLEM

Mr. and Mrs. Smith are facing significant estate taxes.

We therefore want to consider:

✓ What the taxes could be today

✓ How the estate might grow and affect the tax burden on the family in the future

For purposes of this case study, we will grow the Smiths' estate by 5% a year and base the tax impact on that of a married couple.

The chart below illustrates the asset growth and estate tax impact over the next 20 years:*

Year	Estate Size	Federal Estate Taxes
2021	$100,000,000	$31,000,000
2031	$163,000,000	$59,000,000
2041	$265,000,000	$98,000,000

* Figures are rounded to the nearest million

At these levels, Mr. and Mrs. Smith are strongly motivated to take serious steps to reduce the current and projected tax burden.

SOLUTION

We designed a Wealth Preservation and Wealth Transfer Plan that could dramatically reduce the potential future taxes on the Smiths' estate, thereby increasing the wealth transferred from the current generation to the next, and beyond. We implemented the plan in the following five step approach:

Step 1
Implement Two (2) Spousal Lifetime Access Trusts (SLATs)

The SLAT is a multigenerational trust that is typically established in a jurisdiction that has no rule against limiting the duration of the trust. When properly established and administered, a separate SLAT for each family member can conserve family wealth through successive generations (in perpetuity) and substantially minimize taxes upon the transfer of wealth. Almost any type of asset can be gifted, including marketable securities, real estate, business interests or life insurance.

Using a SLAT, the Grantor of the trust can then make gifts to the trust using:

✓ The annual exclusion, currently set at $15,000 per person per year, and/or

✓ The lifetime exemption, currently set at $11,700,000, during the Grantor's lifetime or upon Grantor's death.

Mr. Smith established a trust with his wife, as a lifetime beneficiary and Mrs. Smith established a similar trust with Mr. Smith as a lifetime beneficiary. These trusts will then receive the assets that are to be transferred. From that point forward, Mrs. Smith can receive withdrawals as needed as the beneficiary of Mr. Smith's SLAT, and he can receive distributions as beneficiary of her SLAT.

This addresses the two main concerns of Mr. and Mrs. Smith:

✓ Their income and lifestyle have not been affected.

✓ They have maintained control of the assets.

The SLATs cannot be mirror images of each other. There must be some significant differences in the provisions or the beneficiaries in order to satisfy the IRS that these are real gifts and not a subterfuge to evade taxes. If done correctly, this technique works to move assets out of your estate for tax purposes while keeping control of those assets through your spouse.

Naturally, some people wonder what would happen in the event of a divorce. In the most common design, an equal amount of assets are given to each of the husband's and wife's SLAT. As a practical matter, each spouse would end up with half of the gifted assets thus putting them in the same position as most post divorced couples. Obviously, this strategy is not for every family, which is why every element of every plan must be tailored to the specific family situation.

Step 2
Form A Gifting Entity

A gifting entity is formed by establishing a Family Investment LLC to own the business and real estate. Mr. and Mrs. Smith contribute their closely held business and investments into the LLC. As a result, they each own a 50% interest in the LLC. The LLC operating agreement names Mr. and Mrs. Smith as managers, giving them not only ownership, but control of the LLC.

In order to allow gifting flexibility while maintaining control of the property, we employ managing and non-managing shares. Mr. and Mrs. Smith have the ability to give away non-managing shares, while still retaining control of the LLC by owning the managing shares. Here again, this addresses one of Mr. and Mrs. Smith's main concerns, maintaining control of the business.

Many business owners own the real estate that their business occupies and may even own other income-producing properties. We recommend that any rental property be owned within an LLC for liability protection purposes. Each individual LLC or business entity can be rolled up into a master Family Investment LLC. In this case, if there is any kind of lawsuit resulting from slips and falls or some other type of property ownership liability, the only assets that would be at risk in a lawsuit would be the assets held within that particular LLC.

Step 3
Complete A Formal Valuation

Now that we have created the means to make transfers of non-managing shares of the LLC, we leveraged this technique further by taking a valuation discount. In this context, non-managing, non-controlling, and non-marketable shares are, by definition, less valuable!

A certified valuation analyst was engaged to value a minority, non-controlling interest into the two (2) trusts that were established in Step 1. In this case, we assume that Mr. and Mrs. Smith contributed their entire net worth to the LLC. The analysis determined that the total discount was 30% of the gross asset value. Therefore, after discounts, the LLC was valued at $70 million, for estate tax calculation purposes.

LLC Full Value:	$100 million
LLC Discounted Value:	$70 million

When establishing the value of a gift or transfer for estate tax purposes, the IRS recognizes the limitations of non-voting or non-managing shares, because they are passive and do not allow the owner(s) of these types of shares to control or make important business or financial decisions. Therefore, significant discounts for a non-managing and non-marketable business interest can be realized, from a tax burden standpoint.

Step 4
Gift and Sell the LLC Interests to the SLATs in Two Phases

PHASE 1

Mr. and Mrs. Smith used their lifetime tax exemptions of $11,700,000 each, to transfer a portion of their LLC interests into their respective SLATs. In 2021, the maximum federal exemption is $11,700,000 for individuals ($23,400,000 for married couples).

PHASE 2

Mr. and Mrs. Smith sold their remaining LLC interest totaling approximately $47 million to their respective SLATS and took back a note.

The estate has now been reduced to $70 million for estate tax calculations, with the growth transferred to the trusts. This effectively accomplishing an estate freeze, with only a $47 million note being left in the estate, amortized and paid off over 20 years.

The trust will make payments to the Smiths of $2,852,223 each year for 20 years to support their lifestyle. Here again, we have addressed one of their main concerns. In this example, for 2021, the long term applicable federal interest rate is 1.92%. This is the rate used to calculate interest on the $47 million note. Lower is better, which allows more money to accumulate in the trust, estate tax free.

The critical point to be made here, is that although you are using a discount for estate tax purposes, the actual value of the business and the real estate remains intact and preserved, and all future growth of these assets remains out of your estate for estate tax purposes.

Step 5
Implement Insurance For Asset Replacement and Estate Tax Payments

This step addresses the concern of a premature death, in which the surviving spouse would lose access to the assets that he/she transferred into the trust of which the deceased spouse was a lifetime beneficiary.

To protect each spouse against this scenario, we implemented a $50 million life insurance plan for both Mr. and Mrs. Smith. Assuming, in this example, that Mr. Smith dies prematurely, Mrs. Smith, who is the lifetime beneficiary of his trust, would receive the $50 million death benefit. In effect, the death benefit proceeds replace the lost access to the investment assets previously available when Mr. Smith was alive.

The life insurance premium will be paid from the income on the LLC interests transferred into the trust. The death benefit proceeds are received both income and estate tax free. In addition, this money will continue to grow estate tax free through generations to come, in the SLATs.

CONCLUSION

By designing and implementing a Wealth Preservation and Transfer Plan using Advanced Planning Techniques, we were able to accomplish the Smiths' objectives while addressing their main concerns. The results are summarized below:

- ✓ Assets associated with growth were transferred out of the estate in an extremely tax effective manner, while providing asset protection for Smith family generations to come.

- ✓ The Smiths were able to maintain access to and control of their assets, as lifetime beneficiaries.

- ✓ Estate Tax savings will be in excess of $60 million by the year 2040.

- ✓ Net Increase in Assets to be passed to the Smiths' family members total approximately $80 to $115 million, depending on the year of death.

In this case study, the overall Wealth Preservation and Transfer planning strategies and tools we have highlighted are fairly straight forward and well tested.

However, it is critical to tailor a Wealth Management Plan to a Family's specific and unique situation and needs, and to design and implement the planning tools in the right way. It can make a substantial, multi-million-dollar difference, and may make the difference between keeping the business in the family or not.

Conclusion

360° Family Wealth Management

Throughout this book, we have used a combination of case studies, and in-depth examination of the various planning tools, strategies and techniques that can be employed to help reduce or even eliminate the potential damaging effects of poor wealth preservation and wealth transfer planning. A comprehensive and successful Wealth Management Plan must take into account the following key factors:

- ✓ Wealth Management, for families of considerable wealth, is often a multi-step, complex process.

- ✓ Wealth Management requires significant expertise in several different areas.

- ✓ Wealth Management requires substantial administration.

- ✓ Wealth Management often involves putting together an expert team of advisors, led by a qualified 360° Wealth Manager whose job is to coordinate the team to achieve the desired results.

- ✓ Wealth Management laws, rules and tax exemptions change often, and therefore it is critical that your 360° Wealth Manager helps you stay on top of the changes and modifications required on a regular basis.

- ✓ Wealth Management requires regular maintenance and built-in flexibility in order to keep your plan on track, and to accommodate changing family dynamics and other life circumstances over time.

- ✓ Wealth Management strategies are not a one size fits all. Every element must be tailored to the specific family situation.

It is for these reasons, that we believe that 360° Wealth Management is critical to achieving a successful Family Wealth Management Plan.

Are you a candidate for our 360° Family Wealth Management Services?

Start by taking the 360° Stress Test on the following pages! Once you have a thorough understanding of your current position and the potential costly pitfalls that may lie in wait, you can then decide what actions you may want to consider as you look towards the future.

Take The 360° Stress Test

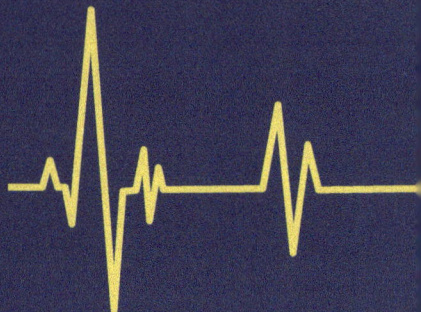

WEALTH PRESERVATION & TRANSFER PLANNING

- ☐ Has your Will been updated in the last five (5) years?
- ☐ Does your Will protect your assets from future divorces, remarriages, or lawsuits?
- ☐ Have you fully implemented all available wealth transfer strategies?
- ☐ Do you know what your estate tax liability is?
- ☐ Do you have enough liquid assets to pay your estate taxes?

BUSINESS SUCCESSION AND EXIT PLANNING

- ☐ Is there a strategy to transfer the business to the next generation in a tax efficient manner?
- ☐ If there is more than one shareholder, is there a Shareholder's Agreement?
- ☐ Does the agreement address death, disability, divorce, disagreement or retirement?
- ☐ Is there a Certificate establishing the value of the business?

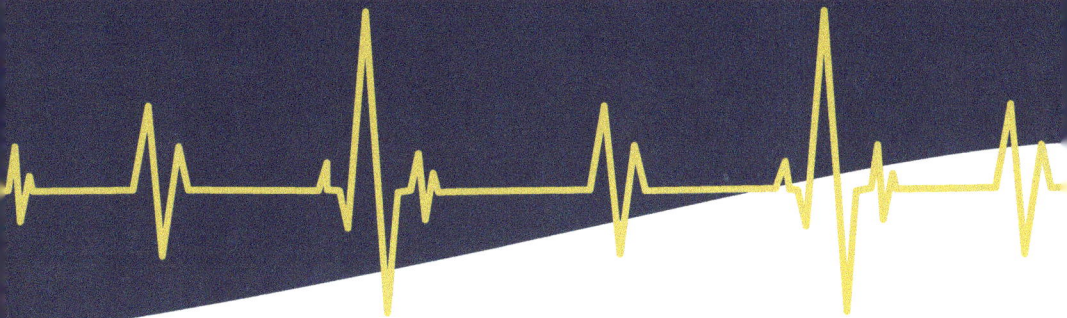

INSURANCE MANAGEMENT

☐ Have all of your life insurance policies been issued within the last five (5) years?

☐ Have you reviewed your life insurance policies in the last five (5) years to determine if additional premiums are required?

☐ Is your insurance properly structured to avoid income and estate taxes?

☐ Is your net worth or family situation unchanged since the policies were issued?

INVESTMENT PLANNING

☐ Do you know how much money you need from the portfolio to maintain your lifestyle?

☐ Is your investment portfolio appropriately allocated based on your objectives, time horizon and risk tolerance?

☐ Are you properly diversified?

☐ Do you regularly review your investment portfolio to harvest tax losses, rebalance and adapt to changing market conditions?

Take the 360° Stress Test online and get an instant score!
https://wealthpreservationsolutions.com/stress-test

About the Authors

ABOUT KEVIN ELLMAN, CFP

As CEO of Wealth Preservation Solutions, Kevin oversees asset management for private wealth clients. He has provided wealth management and planning services to families and business owners for over 30 years.

Kevin has appeared as a financial commentator on CNBC (Morning Call, Portfolio Make-Over, Make Your Money Work, Power Lunch), on ABC and has been quoted in Business Weekly, CBS Market Watch, Fortune Magazine and The Wall Street Journal.

Prior to entering the business of wealth management, Kevin was the Executive Vice President of Beefsteak Charlies, a 70-unit restaurant chain. Early in his career, Kevin was a professional drummer, who toured and recorded with major stars such as: Bette Midler, Barry Manilow, Richie Havens, Todd Rundgren, Mary Travers, and Manhattan Transfer.

Outside the office, Kevin is an avid reader, a fitness buff, and a devoted family man. He enjoys spending his spare time playing golf, scuba diving, and playing music.

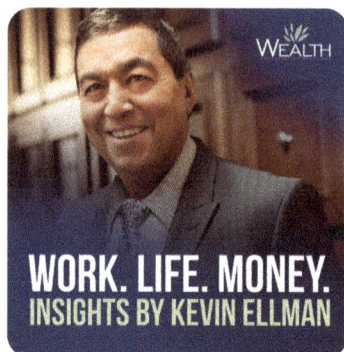

Visit our website for the latest Videos and Podcast episodes
WORK. LIFE. MONEY. Insights with Kevin Ellman
https://wealthpreservationsolutions.com

ABOUT PAUL MILLER

As President of Wealth Preservation Solutions, Paul oversees the Wealth Preservation and Business Succession Planning for the firm's clients. He often serves as an expert resource, authoring various articles on wealth preservation and transfer planning, business succession and exit planning. Paul is a frequent speaker at private industry and association conferences and has appeared as a guest financial commentator on CNBC.

In addition to his activities at the firm, Paul is on the Ramapo College Board of Governors and was a founding trustee of the Ramsey Public Education Foundation. He also represents the Daniell Family Foundation in identifying and supporting New York and New Jersey based charitable organizations.

Paul is a graduate of Boston College, an avid golfer, and a devoted family man.

360° *Family Wealth Management*

Are you a candidate for our 360° Family Wealth Management Services?

If so, feel free to contact us to discuss next steps!

wealthpreservationsolutions.com

A Personal Family Office

WEALTH
PRESERVATION SOLUTIONS

CPSIA information can be obtained
at www.ICGtesting.com
Printed in the USA
JSHW032040230321
12842JS00003B/5

9 780578 867632